Northern Ro

Garry Ward

© 2008 Venture Publications Ltd
ISBN 978 1905 304

Contents

Title Page: Two further Bedford SBGs, along with two Bedford SBOs were acquired in 1957/8, all second-hand, the SBO being the diesel engined version of the Bedford SB, fitted with a Perkins engine. The two SBGs were purchased, almost new, from Smiths of Wigan and a year old SBO came from Yuille of Larkhall. The fourth vehicle was JVD 623, a Bedford SBO with Duple Super Vega 36-seat bodywork which, ironically, had been exhibited in at the 1953 Scottish Motor Show in Northern Roadways livery as depicted here. At less than £3,300, it presented good value for a new light weight coach, but by then, Northern were reducing their coaching operations. The vehicle was delivered instead to Hutchison of Overtown, Lanarkshire, from whom Northern obtained the vehicle in 1957. It ran for three years before its sale in 1960.

Introduction

The former Glasgow independent bus and coach operator, Northern Roadways Ltd, was well known to many, although it existed for less than 40 years. Those years were eventful, involving them in many aspects of bus and coach operation ranging from operating stage carriage services, tours and hire work to running a large scale contract fleet. However, for many, it is probably best known as the operator of prestigious long distance express coach services, commemorated by Corgi in more recent times with the production of a 1/50 scale model of one of their famous Burlingham Seagull-bodied coaches.

The company attracted considerable media attention and captured the imagination of the public during the start up of its express services, yet remarkably little has been documented about it. Much previously unknown information has been uncovered, relating not just to its all too brief high profile express service operations which were, arguably, ahead of their time, but also to the operations preceding and subsequent to these services. The importance of the express services is reflected in the focus of the text, along with the context in which their competitors operated and the events subsequent to the takeover of this portion of the business by the Scottish Bus Group.

Whilst the book is not a definitive history, it provides a fairly detailed (and sometimes complex) story of the company and its activities and a summary of the large variety of vehicles it operated. It is hoped that the reader will find interest in the pages that follow and, perhaps, it may stir memories in older readers who may be able to fill gaps in the story. If it does, the author would be delighted to hear from them.

The Foundations

The company was founded during a particularly dark period of the war, in 1941, Northern Roadways Ltd being incorporated on 20th June of that year, initially with a registered office of 150 Hope Street, Glasgow and a share capital of £2,000, 650 shares being allocated, of which two members of the McGhee family originally held 200. Harry McGhee, a Glasgow solicitor and Nimmo Gardner Napier, who had a chain of retail stores, were the founders of the company. Their initial business was the provision of contract services for the carriage of workers to Government and other factories, major customers being the United States Air Force and the Admiralty.

The Registered office moved in October 1942 to 20 Renfield Street, Glasgow, from which the associated Travel Agency, Travel Trips Ltd, later operated (the latter having been incorporated on 25th February 1946). However, at one time, the company had offices in such diverse locations as Carlisle, Liverpool and Norwich. McGhee's solicitor's office was conveniently positioned above the travel agency office in Glasgow, and the registered office of Northern Roadways moved as he moved premises. A small assortment of elderly Albion and Leyland single-deckers made up Northern's early vehicles. However, few vehicles were owned directly in the early days, vehicles being hired from operators such as Manchester Corporation (seven TS2s, one TS1 and 3 TD1s) and London Transport (nine STs). The STs were operated during the period June 1943 to August 1944 by the company; they received six which had been hired out to Central SMT and three which had operated for Young's Bus Service of Paisley. Indeed, one of the batch was de-roofed whilst in operation with Northern Roadways and had to be fitted with a new top deck to utility specifications. During the war a Glasgow base was established, with vehicles garaged in a lane between the Plaza Ballroom and McNee's Public Bar at Eglington Toll, close to the centre of Glasgow. One of the earliest vehicles recollected as being seen there was a loaned London Transport ST.

Despite the company being a newcomer to the road transport scene, the provision of vital war transport allowed them to apply for and obtain an allocation of new vehicles. A substantial fleet of 16 Bedford OWBs with both Duple and SMT bodywork was obtained. Five were also acquired, nominally second-hand, from Alexanders, although they do not appear to have been used by the latter company. Three further examples were also obtained, this time confirmed 'used' examples, via Millburn Motors, the Glasgow commercial vehicle dealer, having previously been operated by Western SMT.

Neither McGhee or Napier had any previous experience of running passenger transport but they recruited an experienced General Manager in 1944,

Most of the vehicles originally operated by Northern Roadways were hired, including nine London Transport STs. No pictures are known to exist of them in operation with Northern but GH 3854 (ST 512) is pictured here on loan to Young's Bus Service of Paisley, from whom it passed, together with GH 583 and GO 659 (ST 279 and 760 respectively) to Northern in June 1943. *(WJ Haynes)*

Six of the STs came on loan via Central SMT (GN 2095, GK 6246, 6296, GP 6230, GK 5343 and GK 1004, ST 670, 970, 1020, 1026, 530 and 928, respectively). GK 5343 required a roof rebuild by Pickering of Wishaw to utility specifications, whilst operating with Northern as a result of a bridge accident. It remained unique in this respect and is photographed back in operation with London Transport a few weeks before its withdrawal, in February 1949. *(Alan B Cross)*

Supplementing the Bedford OWBs and the hired vehicles were a small motley collection of second-hand Leyland and Albion single-deckers. WH 2377, a Leyland Tiger TS1, with Duple coachwork was new in 1930 and had been acquired from the Lanarkshire operator, Jackson of Auchenheath. It carried the original brown livery, together with the 'Northern' scroll fleetname which was to feature on the side of many vehicles operated for the next 20 years. (*Ian Maclean Collection*)

The first new (and nearly new) vehicles purchased were Bedford OWBs, with a mix of Duple and SMT bodies. Allocations of these vehicles were made possible because of Northern's important role of providing transport for military personnel. AMS 328 had been registered but not used by W Alexander and Son and, in common with others of the batch, had a long life by Northern's standards, operating from 1945 until its sale in 1954. It is seen here in the later silver and blue livery, albeit without an offside fleet name. Buses of this type were used on a wide range of duties, ranging from transport of staff within the Royal Navy Armaments Depot at Beith to (in early post war days) operating private hires.

John Crawford, who had operated buses, with his brother, between Cambuslang and Wishaw before selling out to Glasgow General Omnibus Company, which later became Central SMT in 1932. Under this management, the fleet of company-owned vehicles grew rapidly after the war. Encouraged by the post-war boom in demand for travel, new vehicles were sourced from a variety of chassis and body suppliers. Private hire and touring work quickly became an important source of revenue, much of it generated and supported through the twin valuable assets of their associated Travel Trips Ltd travel agency and the large Ben Wyvis Hotel at Strathpeffer in the Highlands of Scotland, in both of which McGhee had a substantial interest.

Licences were applied for in October 1946 to operate Strathpeffer tours based on the hotel, operating from Blytheswood Square, Glasgow and The Mound, Edinburgh. The applications were initially refused, in January 1947, but Northern appealed and the decision was eventually reversed in October 1947 after a successful application to the Minister of Transport, allowing the operation of up to seven coaches from Glasgow and three from Edinburgh, the terminus of the latter having been changed to Queen Street. The tours, which remained an important part of their operations until the company's demise, used Strathpeffer as a base, operating different 'fantail' trips each day. It is understood that McGhee bought into further hotel interests in the Strathpeffer area as well.

However, contract work also remained an important source of revenue. Construction work commenced on Loch Sloy Hydro Electric scheme in 1945 near Loch Lomond. Northern Roadways gained the contract for transporting the workers to this development, which came on stream in 1951, buses accessing this remote site from Inveruglass on Loch Lomond side.

Military work remained important as well, and in December 1946 they were granted a series of express services for workers from the Royal Navy Armaments Depot at Beith to a number of surrounding towns including Kilmarnock (Railway Station) via Dunlop and Stewarton, returning via Kilmaurs, Torranyard and Burnhouse, two routes to Dalry (Cross) via Kilbirnie and Den, a short route to the small village of Barrmill and others to Gateside, Lochwinnoch and Giffen. The Bedford OBs and OWBs and a couple of Commer Commandos were operated on this contract.

Apparently, the terms of the contract required that the drivers and their vehicles remained at the RNAD depot throughout the day, in case of the need to evacuate the employees quickly, some ten vehicles being employed on the contract. Three vehicles were employed within the complex to transport staff and mail between buildings. A licence was also held for a service between Saltcoats and Giffen where a Ministry of Supply depot was located, which was cancelled a few years later in July 1950, the service being replaced by Western SMT.

Rapid Growth in Glasgow and Ayrshire

The share capital was increased to £12,000 in January 1947 and Napier increased his shareholding substantially in 1949. After the war new vehicles were purchased from wherever the company could get them, with little thought for any standardisation. Northern must have forward-ordered vehicles during the war as they were able to obtain a reasonable quantity of new vehicles within the first two years after the end of the conflict. In 1946, they took delivery of five AEC Regals with Duple C33F bodies, followed in 1947 by seven more. The momentum continued in the next two years with no less than 22 Bedford OBs appearing, with a mixture of Duple and SMT bodies and one with bodywork by McLennan of Spittalfield, who supplied them with four of the OBs second-hand in 1947, plus two second-hand ones from Scout of Preston. The variety of chassis and bodywork combinations was particularly noticeable during this period with two AEC Regals arriving with Northern's first examples of Scottish Aviation 32-seater coach bodywork and two further Regals carrying bodywork by another small local coachbuilder, Stewart of Newmains. Two Commers were purchased, with 29-seater coach bodies built by another Scottish coachbuilder, Croft of Glasgow. Daimler contributed twelve CVD6s with Plaxton C32F bodywork and Maudslay supplied eleven Marathon IIIs, two with Duple C32F bodies, two with Plaxton C33F bodies and seven with 33-seater bodies by Whitson, to a style which closely resembled the Duple 'A' type style of coachwork. One Crossley with Scottish Aviation

Delivery of new heavy-weight vehicles to peace time standards commenced in 1946 with the delivery of five Duple-bodied AEC Regals, seating 33 passengers. EGB 661 is posed at Prestwick Airport with a KLM Royal Dutch Airlines plane from Amsterdam which operated via Prestwick to New York. Although the destination is set for this carrier, the KLM service was primarily provided by Western SMT, both operators giving express service connections to and from Glasgow for the growing number of flights arriving at Prestwick, which had been designated as Britain's second International Airport in April 1946. Knowledge of the facilities provided by airlines was to be the catalyst for the development of a new level of express coach services some five years later. *(Robert Grieves Collection)*

One of the Bedford OWBs delivered new in 1945 was re-bodied with a new Duple Vista 29-seater coach body a year later, giving it the appearance of a Bedford OB. This was followed by batches of Bedford OBs in the period 1947-50. DUS 677 has its destination set for 'Scottish Airlines Prestwick Airport'. Northern also held a licence for a day tour to Prestwick Airport from Glasgow which was popular in the days when transatlantic air travel from Scotland was still very much a novelty. Bedford OBs were also used on the Strathpeffer range of tours, based on the associated Ben Wyvis Hotel. *(Robert Grieves Collection)*

As well as new Bedford OBs, two 'nearly new' examples built in 1947 were acquired from Scout of Preston in the following year (BCK 329 and BCK 535). The first of these is pictured outside the distinctive Ayr Pavilion near the sea front on a private hire; Ayr was a popular destination from Glasgow for day trips. Bedford OBs were also traded with A&C McLennan of Spittalfield in the late 1940s and early 1950s, at least seven being sold to them, whilst four ex-McLennan vehicles were bought in 1947 (BES 789, 790, 973 and BGS 536) some of them having uncommon bodywork by Cadogan of Perth. *(Robert Grieves Collection)*

FGG 171 was the first of two examples with Scottish Aviation bodywork taken into the fleet on AEC Regal chassis in 1948 and is the vehicle to the far left photographed in the works, which were based at Prestwick Airport, probably with the other vehicle, FGG 173 to its right, along with two other vehicles in build (a Foden and an unidentified chassis, possibly another Foden). *(Robert Grieves Collection)*

FGG 171 after delivery, carrying the fixed illuminated plates over the destination boxes, showing 'Northern' and 'Private'. A pre-delivery view shows that the nearside box had been built to accommodate a destination blind but Northern opted for the fixed plate, as they appear to have been principally used on private hire work. Whilst lacking the flowing lines of bodies built by large scale coachbuilders like Plaxton and Duple in that era, they were well liked, Northern describing them as 'most satisfactory' in a commercial press article of the time. Scottish Aviation moved into coach building after the Second World War at a time when civilian aircraft production was at relatively low levels. Adopting skills from the use of alloys in aircraft construction, they produced strong, but relatively light bodies. As an example, Young's Bus Service Maudslays with Scottish Aviation bodies had an unladen weight of 5-19-1, in comparison to similar Brockhouse-bodied machines (albeit, the latter full fronted) of 6-18-3. The coach later passed to Fred Newton of Conan Bridge. *(Garry Ward Collection)*

Two more AEC Regals, also delivered in 1948, carried bodywork by another small coachbuilder, John Stewart of Wishaw. The second vehicle, FGG 174, is pictured outside the coachworks prior to delivery. From the front profile, it bears a resemblance to the Duple A-type body. The winged Northern Roadways motif below the cab window was very unusual, a 'Glengarry' usually being displayed. *(Robert Grieves Collection)*

Although the front and side profile bore some resemblance to the Duple style of the era, the rear view had a look of a prewar Alexander body. Both Stewart-bodied vehicles (FGG 172 and 174) had very short lives, even by Northern's standards, being sold after only a year of service. *(Robert Grieves Collection)*

The hire of a Daimler CVD6 demonstrator was rewarded with orders for twelve Daimler CVD6s with Plaxton 33-seat coach bodies in 1948. These carried the more usual Northern scroll fleet name and 'Glengarry' emblem on the front and side. The delivery of large quantities of coaches allowed Northern to expand their private hire business substantially, facilitated by the associated Travel Trips agency office which was centrally located in Glasgow. GUS 291 had been decorated with star emblems on the radiator and a plate carrying a single 'N', no doubt by its regular proud driver. The practice was quite common in Ayrshire in the 1940s when drivers were allocated their own vehicle, encouraging a sense of pride. *(Robert Grieves Collection)*

Maudslays were popular chassis with Northern Roadways in the early post-war period and there were stories of quantities of them being obtained, then stored in barns until coachbuilders could be found to fit bodies to them. Eleven of this type entered service in 1948, including two with Plaxton bodywork, two with Duple bodies and seven with bodies by Whitson to a style similar to the Duple A-type body. Whitson bodied GGA 932 is turning from Clyde Street onto Glasgow Bridge when new. It operated until 1954. Two similar vehicles (GGA 565 and GGA 656) passed to Northern Ayrshire Coaches and were acquired later with the Irvine area operations by members of the AA consortium.

New vehicles were obtained from a wide variety of manufacturers in small to medium size batches but, even by Northern's standards, the purchase of a Crossley in 1948 was a 'one off' for the time. Bodying by Scottish Aviation made a combination which was even more unusual. The bodywork had similarities with the examples supplied on AEC Regals, but had a much deeper side and front cab window, to suit the lower set Crossley radiator. As with the bodies on the AEC Regals, the Northern fleet name was carried in the coach side trims. GGB 362 is posed new at Prestwick Airport. *(Garry Ward Collection)*

The first double-decker owned (as opposed to hired) was a former Daimler CVD6 demonstrator with Northern Coachbuilders H30/26R bodywork (GHP 259) in 1948, followed by two brand new Daimler CVD6s with H30/26R bodies by Barnard of Norwich, registered GGE 842 and 843 in the following year. These were the only double-deckers bought new and the only ones to carry Barnard bodywork, never a common type in Scotland (Dundee Corporation having the largest quantity of double-deck bodies with 22 as the Barnard publicity indicates). The five bay bodies carried a variation of the silver and blue livery with a swept skirt panel and variation on the standard scroll Northern fleetname. Their purchase is all the more unusual because the parent Northern Roadways had no stage carriage services and they were, effectively, used on contract or private hire work for the four years that they operated in the fleet. Both passed to the Lanarkshire operator, Hutchison of Overtown in 1953. *(Robert Grieves Collection)*

GHP 259 had been a demonstrator for Daimler and visited a number of operators, including Edinburgh Corporation and Bournemouth Corporation, where it is pictured around 1947. After purchase by Northern Roadways in 1948, the vehicle was regularly allocated to the Ayrshire operations of its subsidiary Northern Ayrshire Coaches Ltd, providing works and school transport in the Irvine area, although it remained owned by the parent company, passing to Garelochhead Coach Services in 1953.

Plaxton supplied all but one of the 33-seat bodies on the 1949 batch of Maudslay Marathons. GGD 910 was one of four vehicles later down-seated and fitted with toilets for use on the express services in 1951. Members of this batch of Maudslays, along with the similar 1948 deliveries, were regularly used on the Strathpeffer area tours and also served on the Scarborough express services. They survived until 1953/4. *(Robert Grieves Collection)*

C32F bodywork was also obtained, an uncommon chassis north of the border. During this period, coaches were operated for a couple of years then sold and replaced with new stock.

In 1949 they purchased their only new double-deckers ever owned when two Daimler CVD6 double-deckers with bodywork by another lesser-known coachbuilder, Barnard of Norwich, were obtained. An ex-Daimler CVD6 double-deck demonstrator with Northern Coachbuilders 56-seatbodywork had also been acquired from Daimler in December 1948. Additional contract work had been obtained with the granting of licences in February 1949 for services from Johnstone (Milliken Park Filling Station) to Georgetown (10 AFV Depot) via Linwood and from Glasgow (Carlton Place) to Georgetown via Paisley. However, two licences for services to Georgetown from Paisley (Ferguslie Park and County Square) were refused, Garners of Bridge of Weir successfully obtaining these licences. Substantial Ordnance facilities existed at both Georgetown and Bishopton, the latter still existing today. Northern and Garners of Bridge of Weir covered the transport of workers to the former facility, whilst Western SMT was involved in providing transportation to the latter.

During 1949 ten more Maudslay Marathons were obtained, nine with Plaxton 33-seater bodies and one with Duple 33-seater bodywork. Twelve more Bedford OBs with Duple bodies were bought and 13 33-seater Daimler CVD6s were acquired with Plaxton bodies, some of the latter having full front bodywork.

The livery had originally been brown with a cream band, but changed after the war to an attractive silver grey and blue colour scheme, with a 'Northern' scroll fleet name carried on the side and full fleet name, legal address and phone number carried on the boot. Many vehicles carried twin tartan 'Glengarrys' on either side of the fronts of the vehicles.

Their ability to obtain relatively large numbers of new vehicles early in the post war period caused much consternation to the late William Sword, at that time Assistant Manager of Western SMT (and son of the legendary JC Sword who had formed Midland Bus Service, a major component of Western when it was formed in 1932). Correspondence flowed between Sword and local friends in Renfrewshire, conveying the

concern that Northern were able to advertise vehicles for hire for weddings, for example, whilst Western struggled to upgrade its service bus fleet. Northern's lack of stage carriage work meant that vehicles could be allocated to private hire work, when not needed for contracts. For example, three wooden seated Bedford OWBs were used on a Womens Guild annual outing from Glasgow to Inverary on one occasion.

The placement of a number of Burlingham-bodied PS1s and AECs into Western's Inchinnan garage as early as possible in 1948 was an attempt to re-gain or at least share some of this private hire market. William Sword recounted to me some years ago how he learned that Northern obtained quantities of Maudslay chassis, storing them under hay in barns at various farms until coachbuilders could be found to body them. Northern's ability to obtain large numbers of new vehicles also worried their staff, a former office member telling me how they often wondered whether their wages would be paid that week, every time a new vehicle appeared on the road. Payment to creditors was known to be rather slow at times.

Northern's early post war expansion had concentrated on coaching and contract work but in April 1949 they created a subsidiary company with similar name to its parent and the same legal address of 20 Renfield Street, Glasgow, named Northern Ayrshire Coaches Ltd. This company had been formed to take over the business of Walker's Garage Limited of 25 Main Street, Kilbirnie. Walker's had a stage carriage service from Kilbirnie (Maybole Bridge) to Beith (Strand) which they acquired, together with garage premises at the latter location. They also held a schools contract service from Lochwinnoch Cross to Beith (Spiers School), Kilbirnie Institute to Beith (Strand) and excursions and tours licences from both Kilbirnie and Beith. Vehicles had run in a livery of purple (or royal blue) and grey, relieved by a cream roof and window surrounds. The Kilbirnie to Beith service had its terminal points altered to Lynn Drive and Auldlea Road in April 1950 respectively.

Northern's rapid expansion came to the attention of Glasgow Corporation who, in 1949, found themselves short of vehicles to maintain certain duties. McGhee was even approached to determine if Northern Roadways could provide evening peak period coverage for up to 16 services, with an estimated vehicle utilisation of some 40 buses. It would appear that nothing came of this interesting proposition, their requirement probably coinciding with a busy period of the day for Northern's fleet, together with the Corporation's varied requirements. As an example of their requirements, Service 11 from Hope Street to Provanmill or Robroyston required two buses between the period of 3:59pm and 6:21pm. Service 23 from Shawlands or Peat Road to Govan Cross required four buses between 4:31pm and 6:44pm. Some years later an approach was made in the reverse by Northern to Glasgow Corporation, offering to assist with drivers and buses, of which more anon.

Meanwhile, they were looking to develop another arm of their business and applied in December 1949 for licences for extended tours from both Glasgow and Edinburgh to Paris (9 days), the French and Italian Riviera and Paris (16 days) and Rome (20 days). Two established operators of Continental tours, Cotters of Glasgow and McKelvie of Barrhead, objected, together with Western SMT, although the latter company only operated licensed British tours. The licences were refused in March 1950 and no further attempt was made to expand into this area of the market.

In May 1949, they acquired a second business, James Hicks (Motor Hirers) of 34 Prestwick Road, Ayr, and incorporated their operations into Northern Ayrshire Coaches Ltd. Hicks had acquired the business of William Love of Irvine earlier in the year, Love having operated an Irvine (Clark Drive at Allan Square) to Kilwinning (Braidwood Avenue) service, via Ravenspark Hospital and Blacklands. A second licence was held for carrying workers from Irvine (Clark Drive) to the Royal Ordnance Factory on the northern outskirts of the town and the licences were granted in July 1949.

Hicks' vehicles operated in a red livery with cream window surrounds and roof and a green waistband, large fleet names being carried in gold. It is believed that Hicks was appointed the manager of Northern Ayrshire Coaches Ltd. These acquisitions gave Northern a valuable foothold in Ayrshire, in the heart of the area of the A1 and AA Co-operative area of operations and, to an extent, Western SMT. As well as the depot at Beith inherited with Walker's business,

Northern Ayrshire Coaches had a depot in Irvine, in the old Fullerton Street area. Northern Ayrshire Coaches also parked up a couple of vehicles in Aitken Street, Dalry overnight (two Whitson-bodied Maudslays are remembered GGA 565, 656 from the parent company), probably to assist in servicing the RNAD contract. The two Barnard-bodied Daimler CVD6 double-deckers and the Northern Coachbuilders-bodied Daimler CVD6 from the parent fleet were also regularly used on school contracts around Irvine. Vehicles operated primarily in the same livery as the parent company, although Bedford OWBs ran in all grey whilst four ex-Chesterfield Leyland Tigers operated in a dark blue livery.

The sister Northern Ayrshire Coachways applied in January 1950 for a daily works service, Mondays to Saturday, between Kilwinning (Caley Station) and Kilmarnock (Moorfield Estate) via Irvine, but the licence was refused in May 1950. More successful was the application in March 1950 for a daily return service for workers between Irvine Cross and the Georgetown RAOC complex in Renfrewshire, operating via Beith, Howwood and Elderslie, which was granted in May. An application for an extension of their Irvine service further along Clark Drive was refused in April 1950, no doubt due to objections from AA. Irvine Town Council were anxious to have a comprehensive service within the town and Northern were keen to oblige, as there had been problems of passengers being left on the Clark Drive route on which both AA and Northern operated, as well as on the MacKinlay Crescent service. After the refusal of their application, a meeting was arranged between Western SMT, A1, AA and Northern at the promptings of the Town Council, but unfortunately Northern did not attend and AA were of the view that the other three operators should work together. However, in the meantime, Northern were granted permission to increase the frequency of their Irvine to Kilwinning service to half hourly. Continued prompting by Irvine Town Council for a service to Drybridge particularly concerned AA as they believed Northern could apply to extend their Irvine local service to meet this need over part of an AA route.

Countering the move, AA applied for a service between Drybridge and Irvine Mains Housing Scheme (Livingstone Terrace) in March 1951.

To support the Northern Ayrshire Coaches' operations four former Chesterfield Leyland Tigers were purchased, two Leyland TS7s (CRA 264 and 266) with Metro-Cammell B32 bodies and two TS8s with Leyland B32R bodywork (ERA 90 and 91). Newly acquired ERA 91 was photographed near Irvine Cross in June 1950, having passed to Northern from Irvine of Salsburgh, apparently with an 'on hire' sticker in the nearside front window, operating on the Irvine (Clark Drive) to Kilwinning (Braidwood Avenue) service. All four ran in a dark blue livery (similar in shade to that used by East Yorkshire) and carried 'Northern Ayrshire Coaches' fleet name at the rear. The two TS7s passed to Garnock Valley with the acquisition of the Beith operations, whilst the TS8s passed to AA Motor Services when the Irvine area operations were taken over in August 1953, ERA 91 quickly passing to a contractor from the AA partner, Young's of Ayr. *(Alan B Cross)*

However, vying for new routes within Irvine continued between the operators. Parent Northern Roadways had suggested to the Town Council that they were prepared to operate a service from Winton Road to Rubie Crescent over the AA route, as this area was heavily populated. This would compete with the Irvine local section of the newly applied for Drybridge route and Northern gained the upper hand by obtaining the Town Council's support for the application they planned to make. A formal application was made in April 1951 for a service between Rubie Crescent and Livingstone Terrace, and the application was granted in December 1951, despite objections. AA Motor Services appealed, but were unsuccessful and were ordered to pay costs in August 1952. Despite the objections and counter objections to services, A1, AA, Western and Northern Ayrshire reached agreement on fares coordination in November 1951.

Fleet expansion continued, but at a temporarily slower pace; six more Bedford OBs, three with

Duple and three with Plaxton bodies were obtained in 1950. In September 1950, a new excursion and tour licence was applied for from Glasgow to Colintraive via Loch Lomond and Strachur on the outward journey and via Arrochar and Helensburgh inbound, which was granted in December 1950, replacing a similar earlier licence. In April of the following year, they applied for a service between Pollok (Bundy Clock) and Glasgow (Kerr Street), to operate as a works service under contract to the carpet factory of J Templeton and Company (a spectacular building, incidentally, modelled on the Doges Palace), using double-deckers. The service was granted, initially under short term licences, and then granted as a full licence in August 1951.

McGhee and Napier continued to look for other companies as possible acquisition candidates. Their meteoric growth is known to have attracted the attention of the A1 combine at a time when there was uncertainty around the full extent of the nationalisation of the bus industry intended by the

Labour Government of the day. This resulted in Northern being approached regarding their possible interest in acquiring the bus co-operative. Nothing came of this approach or, for that matter, a later interest which McGhee and Napier had in the business of Yeates of Rothesay around 1954. Harry McGhee lived in Rothesay and is bound to have had some local knowledge of the operator, who had excursion and tours licences as well as a stage carriage route which operated the fearsome climb to Canada Hill, where the Co-operative had a summer camp.

Well-known Barrhead independent McGill's Bus Service acquired the company in 1955 and operated it under the grander title of Rothesay Motor Services. However, one successful takeover was the acquisition of the excursions and tours business of

Northern Roadways and Northern Ayrshire Coaches military, school and main stage services in 1951.

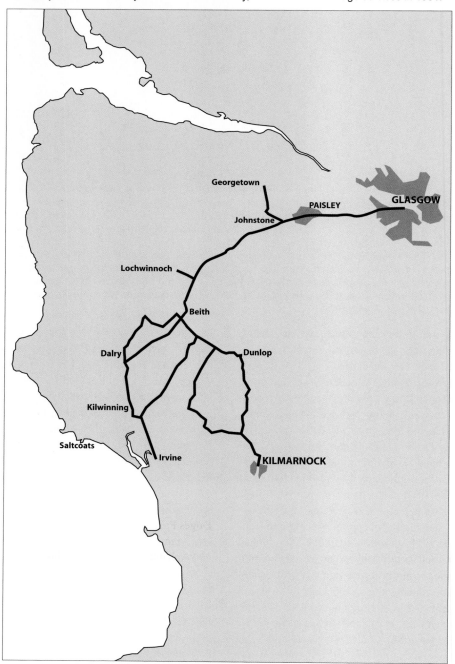

Clydebank Co-operative Society. Despite objections from both Western SMT and Central SMT, the licences were granted in December 1951. Three Crossleys with Scottish Aviation bodies also passed to Northern and were operated alongside Northern's own similar example.

Express Service Development

Northern Roadways had obtained a licence to operate a Glasgow – Prestwick Airport service for the transatlantic air passengers of American Overseas Airways (who later became Pan American Airways), as well as Scottish Aviation and Trans-Canada Airlines in 1946. Passengers who had booked flights through their associated Travel Trips Ltd travel agency were also carried.

Having fulfilled a vital wartime role, Prestwick was officially designated as Britain's second International Airport in April 1946 and air services were developed quickly. Western SMT also obtained a licence to connect with the KLM transatlantic flights from Amsterdam via Prestwick to New York and provided connections for another carrier, SAS, who operated from Scandinavia across the Atlantic. Northern Roadways were granted pick up and setting down points from some of the Glasgow hotels, including the Beresford, as well as Kilmarnock Railway Station. This relatively small development was the catalyst for greater things. The commercial transport press later reported that the standard of comfort provided on these airline services gave Napier and McGhee the idea of providing a similar concept on express road services. The thinking was to provide a fleet of luxury coaches with toilets and reclining seats, with trained hostesses supplying light meals throughout the long journeys. At that time, coaches were still limited to a speed of 30mph and existing services like the Western SMT Glasgow-London express service were taking nearly 16 hours. Whilst Western used comfortable vehicles, seats were fixed and no vehicles had toilets. Refreshment stops were made at pre-arranged locations which could often be overrun when a convoy of vehicles arrived at similar times.

Northern lodged a comprehensive set of applications with the Traffic Commissioners in October 1950 for a range of express services as follows;

From Glasgow (Blytheswood Square) to London (Victoria Coach Station) via Carlisle and Doncaster, picking up and setting down at Glasgow, Hamilton, Lockerbie and London and between Edinburgh (Queen Street) and London (Victoria Coach Station) via Hawick and Carlisle, picking up and setting down at Edinburgh, Hawick and London. Operation of up to nine vehicles was requested.

From both Glasgow and Edinburgh to Liverpool (St Johns Lane) via Carlisle, Kendal, Lancaster and Preston, picking up and setting down at Glasgow, Hamilton, Lockerbie and Liverpool and for the Edinburgh service picking up and setting down at Edinburgh, Hawick and Liverpool, both services to operate with a maximum of six vehicles.

From both Glasgow and Edinburgh to Manchester (East Street Coach Station, close to Lower Mosley Street), following the same route as the Liverpool service, picking up and setting down at Glasgow, Hamilton, Lockerbie and for the Edinburgh service picking up and setting down at Edinburgh, Hawick and Manchester, both services to operate with a maximum of six vehicles.

From both Glasgow and Edinburgh to Birmingham (Smithfield Garage, Digbeth) via Carlisle, Kendal, Lancaster, Preston, Warrington and Whitchurch, picking up and setting down at Glasgow, Hamilton, Lockerbie and Birmingham and for the Edinburgh service picking up and setting down at Edinburgh, Hawick and Birmingham, both services to operate with a maximum of six vehicles.

A summer-only service from both Glasgow and Edinburgh to Scarborough (Crown Garage) via Carlisle, Scotch Corner and York, picking up and setting down in Glasgow and Scarborough only and for the Edinburgh service operating via Hawick, Carlisle, Scotch Corner and York, picking up and setting down in Edinburgh and Scarborough only, both services to operate with a maximum of five vehicles.

Northern also applied for new tours to Grantown on Spey (7 days) and Bridlington (7 days, using a maximum of three vehicles), from both Glasgow and Edinburgh.

Hearings were set for all applications for December 1950. The list of objectors was formidable; SMT, Western SMT, Ribble, Standerwick, Scout, D Lawson Ltd, Lowland Motorways, United Automobile Services and the Railway Executive.

The London service application, in particular, was astutely timed, a few months prior to the scheduled opening of the Festival of Britain Exhibition at Battersea. Demand for travel to this post-war 'feel good' event, to be held between May and September 1951 was predicted to be high, with existing facilities via road or rail unlikely to cater for the demand. Western attempted to placate this situation by requesting sanction to operate four additional vehicles in any one day when required, during the period of the Festival and the primary application was granted in February 1951.

To the astonishment of the Scottish Bus Group and British Railways, the Scottish Licensing Authority granted Northern's primary licences for the London express services in March 1951, allowing up to six vehicles, indicating that Northern Roadways would cater for demand from passengers who thought that rail fares were too high but existing road facilities were not adequate. The London services were very much the 'Jewels in the Crown' of the Scottish Bus Group's SMT company, (who operated various permutations of the Edinburgh to London express service) and, arguably, were even more prestigious from the viewpoint of Western SMT, who operated the Glasgow to London express service. William Sword's father had introduced the first regular direct service from Glasgow to London in the late 'twenties, through his company, Midland Bus Service of Airdrie.

The Glasgow to Scarborough licence and the Glasgow and Edinburgh excursions and tours licences to Bridlington were also granted in March 1951, together with authority to operate the Glasgow to Birmingham service, allowing only two duplicate vehicles and no pick ups within the area. The Edinburgh to Birmingham and Edinburgh to Scarborough applications were refused in the same month. The applications for the Glasgow and Edinburgh services to both Liverpool and Manchester were withdrawn by Northern Roadways in March 1951, perhaps because of the volume of objections and a desire to focus their attention on the licences that had been granted.

During the same period, a company which also incorporated 'Roadways' into its name, Sibbald Roadways of 18 Charlotte Lane, Edinburgh withdrew its ambitious application for express services from both Glasgow and Edinburgh to Northholt (London) Airport and Dover in January 1951 (the month of the Northern hearing), having applied in November 1950. One of their express service applications was similar to a later attempt by Northern Roadways themselves, of which more later. Their Edinburgh service was to have operated via Penicuick, Moffat, Carlisle, Brough, Scotch Corner, Doncaster, Baldock and Mill Hill and the Glasgow service via Abington, Carlisle and then by the same southbound route as the Edinburgh service. The application from both Edinburgh and Glasgow to Dover followed the same route to Northolt, then onward via Ealing, Streatham, Bromley, Maidstone and Folkestone to Dover. Passengers were to be picked up and set down at the terminal points, plus Northolt Airport and Folkestone. Objections were raised by the Railway Executive, SMT, Cotter's Tours, Edinburgh and Glasgow Corporations (for their respective areas).

Returning to Northern, to support their express services, a fleet of 20 underfloor-engined vehicles were ordered for delivery in 1951 in optimistic anticipation of obtaining the licences, in the form of 16 AEC Regal IVs and four Leyland Royal Tigers, all with Burlingham 32-seat luxury coach bodies. These splendid vehicles were equipped with reclining seats, heaters, a radio, toilet compartment with wash hand basin and plug point for electric razor, hot water tank and fold down sink and crockery and food storage areas (placed immediately forward of the toilet compartment on the offside). The toilet compartment and rear window were obscured with leaded light glass in a sunrise pattern. The vehicles were finished in the attractive silver grey and blue livery adopted for the whole fleet post war, finished off with Northern fleet names in chrome on the side panels, a full Northern Roadways legend on the boot, illuminated 'Northern Pullman' panels above the boot door and two tartan 'Glengarrys' on either side of the front panel.

SMT already had Alexander-bodied AEC Regal coaches on order, fitted with 30 reclining seats and a toilet compartment. Fourteen of the batch were hurriedly diverted from their order to Western SMT (with Edinburgh registrations and exterior coach trims to suit the SMT diamond fleet name), to upgrade their London service. At the time, the Western service was largely maintained by Burlingham-bodied Leyland Tiger PS1s,

Sixteen AEC Regal IVs and four Leyland Royal Tigers were ordered with Burlingham 32-seat coach bodies and were registered JGD 110-117, JGE 419-426, the four Leyland Royal Tigers being registered JGE 427-430. The first six AEC Regals (JGD 110-115) were available for commencement of the express services in May 1951 and, prior to the start up, Northern parked one of them, JGD 112, outside the associated Travel Trips Travel Agency in Renfield Street Glasgow to publicise the new services; it appeared to be attracting considerable interest from the public. A Glasgow Corporation tram can be glimpsed in the background. At that time, the Corporation continued to have a very extensive network of tram services within and beyond the Glasgow City boundary, as well as a growing bus fleet, for which Northern Roadways had earlier been asked to discuss possible evening peak hour support. *(Geoff Morrant Collection)*

AEC Regal IV JGD 111 is led into the original Kings Cross Coach Station at Judd Street on its inaugural journey on 7th May 1951, witnessed by members of the public and, evidently, some press. These were the lucky passengers, as Northern had taken bookings on the basis of them being licensed to operate six coaches on each route (although only the first six of the new coaches were available at the start up date, as indicated) and considerable re-booking had to be undertaken when the backing licence subsequently only allowed two. The introduction of underfloor engined vehicles gave coachbuilders the opportunity to produce more flowing attractive designs and Burlingham are widely acknowledged as being one of the most successful with their Seagull design.

JGD 111 is seen again in the unloading area, together with at least two other Northern coaches. AEC Regals JGD 116/7 arrived in June 1951 to boost the front line fleet to eight. The silver and blue livery complimented the elegant design of the coachwork and the batch of 20 vehicles were quickly christened by the commercial press as 'Roadliners'. Both Burlingham and Northern Roadways made good use of the publicity surrounding these vehicles, which were the largest batch of Burlingham Seagull-bodied new vehicles delivered to a Scottish operator.

Leyland Royal Tiger JGE 427, with AEC Regal IV JGE 419 behind are pictured at the Blytheswood Square terminus in April 1953. JGE 419-26 had arrived in July 1951, the four Royal Tigers, JGE 427-30 completing deliveries in August 1951. The specification varied slightly on the Burlingham bodies, possibly dictated by the urgency of obtaining delivery and having to take what was quickly available, these two being fitted with half drop side windows, whereas others had sliding windows. The board just visible in the nearside front window indicated the coach number and its origin or destination in Scotland (G for Glasgow and E for Edinburgh) to assist passengers in identifying their coach. *(John C Gillham)*

supplemented by Maudslay Marathons acquired with the business of Young's Bus Service of Paisley.

From the granting of the primary licences by the Scottish Licensing Authority to the granting of the reduced backing licence for two vehicles on each London service by the Metropolitan Licensing Authority three months later in May, 20,000 applications for bookings on the Northern Roadways services were received. Ever mindful of publicity, Northern Roadways parked one of their new AEC Regal coaches outside the Travel Trips travel agency in Renfield Street a few days prior to the start of the London services on 7th May 1951. Although licensed as 32-seaters, the new Burlingham-bodied vehicles were only 'charted' for 30 passengers, the rear two seats being for the use of the second driver and the hostess. Initially, bookings were not taken from London, such was the demand. Passengers were booked on the basis that the primary licence for six vehicles would be granted rather than the two vehicles which were authorised later. Given the level of bookings, this caused considerable chaos initially as changes had to be made.

At the Glasgow terminus, Northern used a small hut located between two buildings to provide a booking point and position for the regulator to control express service departures. The first coach to London from Glasgow was waved off by the Lord Provost of Glasgow, with driver Jackie Boyd at the wheel. As well as the commercial vehicle press, the new services captured the imagination of the public, with the general press reporting on the new services at the time. Coaches were scheduled to leave Glasgow and Edinburgh at 6:30pm nightly; arriving in London at 10:45am the next day, with return journeys from London leaving at 7:30pm and duly arriving at 11:45am the following day in Glasgow and Edinburgh. The only intermediate pick up point was Hamilton, where Travel Trips had a booking office (and where ten minutes stopover was allowed in either direction), coaches then proceeding to Penrith where they met up with the Edinburgh coaches and a break was taken, drivers changing over at this point.

The Edinburgh to London service was provided by running 'light' from Glasgow, with drivers and hostess to Queen Street, Edinburgh, where passengers were uplifted. In reverse, on arrival from London, the coach would offload passengers, and then run 'light' back to Glasgow. The service operated from Queen Street, near North Castle Street corner (parallel to Princess Street), via Dalkeith, Stow, Galashiels (scheduled 10 minute stop), Hawick (scheduled 10 minutes stop) and Carlisle (scheduled 10 minute stop).

Normally, stops were taken again at Moores' Garage on the north side of Doncaster, where the coach was refuelled and a further break was taken, drivers changing over again and, finally, Alconbury Hill, near Huntingdon, close to an RAF base, where the final stop for breakfast (including a bottle of orange juice) was taken and the last driver changeover was undertaken. The authorised timetable was slightly different, the Glasgow service having scheduled ten minute stops at Lockerbie and Carlisle.

The first return journey north was inaugurated by a short ceremony at the Kings Cross Coach Station, when the 'Mayor and Mayoress of St Pancras', Councillor SJ Williams and Mrs Williams attended the departure and cut a tape to signify the start of the journey by the three coaches heading north. The Glasgow terminus was reached from London via Broomhouse, Mount Vernon, Tollcross Road, Duke Street, George Street and West George Street, then in a circular route via West Campbell Street, West Regent Street and Pitt Street, to finish up facing basically eastwards back in West George Street at a steep section which climbs to Blytheswood Square.

Average loadings on the Glasgow to London service were high and the commercial press reported that by the end of September 1951, 1,584 journeys had been operated on the two London services with over 40,000 passengers carried, with a load factor of over 85%. The transport press carried features on this innovative new service, one of the photographs showing Napier talking to a number of the hostesses, after completion of the maiden trip south to London. The transport press covered the first journey north to Edinburgh, commenting favourably on the facilities provided. Two points were noted, one being the 'ridiculously slow speed of 30mph' which vehicles were legally limited to, (a common complaint for years to come), resulting in drivers having to slow down to keep to the schedule. The other observation was that the coach allocated to the Edinburgh journey had

Penrith was a designated refreshment stop and passengers were encouraged to make use of the facilities in Ernie Hartness' garage, seen behind, to help in avoiding overload of the on board toilet. AEC Regal IV JGE 422 was Edinburgh bound in this early morning view in April 1953 and would divert north of Carlisle onto the A7 to reach its destination via Hawick, whilst Leyland Royal Tiger JGE 427 would continue up the A74 to Glasgow. *(John C Gillham)*

Moore's Garage, a filling station adjacent to the A1 on the northern outskirts of Doncaster, was open 24 hours a day and used for re-fuelling by Northern coaches. AEC Regal IV JGE 420 is showing some signs of use, with a couple of dents in the front panels. *(John C Gillham)*

only been delivered on the day of the first departure, preventing the opportunity for a full examination before the commencement of the first journey and a couple of 'teething troubles' had been spotted; failure of a nearside headlamp bulb and a faulty windscreen wiper.

A smart uniform complete with cap was provided (from the well known outfitters of the time, Paisleys in Jamaica Street, Glasgow) for both the hostesses and the drivers, emphasizing the 'up market' image. Photographs were taken of the first vehicles arriving at Judd Street Coach Station, Kings Cross after their 16 hour journey and Burlingham made good use of this publicity by taking out their own advert, extolling the virtues of these well-equipped vehicles, using the term 'Roadliner' coaches. Ironically, Western had used the same term to describe Leyland Lions which had been rebodied by Brush after the war to resume their own London service. Northern preferred to call the vehicles 'Pullman Deluxe' in their publicity data due, no doubt, to their desire to emphasize a light meal service at your seat but also, possibly, to avoid confusion with the similar Roadways part of their fleet name. Fares were pitched higher than the comparable Western and SOL services to London, a single fare being £2 one way, in comparison to the Scottish Bus Group's £1 10s.

Both Northern and the Scottish Bus Group provided rugs to help to keep passengers warm, but Northern Roadways passengers got pillows and, in the early days, magazines. Hot drinks were provided at various points on the journey, as well as sandwiches from a quality baker in Glasgow, Strachans of Pollokshields, provided on an airline style tray. A 200 watt immersion heater kept the water hot for the drinks, but was a heavy drain on the coach's electrical system and there were occasions when the vehicles could not cope with the strain, producing 'lukewarm' water. The termini used were, perhaps, the least salubrious aspects of the operation; Judd Street was simply a piece of waste land in the Kings Cross area with various sheds around the perimeter at the corner of Cromer Street and Judd Street, permission to use the Victoria Coach Station having been refused. Judd Street terminus closed on 31st December 1953, to allow houses to be built. Northern vehicles then terminated at another site in the area, the Pentonville Road Coach Station, another similar piece of waste land. After unloading

passengers and their luggage, the vehicles were parked up in Judd Street or, on occasion, surrounding streets, and cleaned out internally by the crew, but fuelling was only undertaken at Moores Garage at Doncaster and external coach washing and toilet emptying on the London service was only undertaken at the Glasgow base; the latter could cause problems on occasion.

Passengers were encouraged to make use of facilities at stopping points such as Penrith where the garage facilities of Ernie Hartness were available to mitigate this issue, but there were occasions when passengers' luggage was damaged by overflow from the toilet system, with subsequent claims being made. It was not unknown for Northern drivers to undertake illegal emptying en-route to avoid such problems. Having parked up, crews then made their way to accommodation booked by Northern to allow them some sleep and a meal prior to the return journey. Incidentally, the crew were not paid expenses for dinner, reliance being placed on tips from passengers. Fresh food boxes would be obtained at each terminal point for the return journey.

Western SMT and SMT were both stung into action; one immediate move was to apply for unlimited duplication on Glasgow to Manchester, Blackpool, Liverpool and London services in March 1951. The hearing for the express services unlimited duplication was set for June and Northern Roadways, naturally, objected. A high profile campaign was launched by James Amos, the then Chairman of the Scottish Bus Group of bus companies and in June 1951, both companies were granted permission to increase duplication on the London routes to twelve (thus, thirteen in all) in place of the maximum of four each from 1st June for the period of the Festival of Britain.

The Scottish Bus Group and British Railways Executive were concerned not just at the granting of this particular set of licences, but of the knock-on impact, as they had noted that many companies in Scotland and England had applied for cancellation of their duplicating restrictions or made applications for new services, some of which were reported to have been granted according to Western SMT in a March 1951 meeting. When it became clear that the Metropolitan Traffic Authority would be giving reduced backing to Northern's application, the Scottish Bus Group appealed to the Minister of Transport. By late

The last refreshment stop before London was an old airfield at Alconbury Hill, near Stamford, where a light breakfast was served. Passengers and drivers are 'stretching their legs' outside the two AEC Regals and the Leyland Royal Tiger in this early morning view on a southbound journey. *(Robert Grieves Collection)*

JGE 421 was nearing the end of its 16 hour journey north from London as it ran over the stone setts on the approach to Blytheswood Square, Glasgow. The lack of traffic in this scene will be noted. *(Garry Ward Collection)*

With the granting of additional duplication on the London services in June 1951, Northern had four of the Plaxton-bodied Maudslay Marathons (GGD 910, GUS 294, 815 and 816) , delivered in 1949 converted to 26-seaters and fitted with toilets but without a boiler. GUS 815 has returned north from London and the hostess has already stored the pillows on one of the seats. She would have had a busy night, serving passengers in both the Maudslay and a full size coach. In this case, it was DMS 676 parked behind, an AEC Regal IV with similar Burlingham Seagull coachwork to Northern's own examples, operated from new by Fleming of Bannockburn on contract to Northern and painted in full Northern Roadways livery.

At the other end of the route, another one of the converted Maudslays, GUS 294, sits at London's King Cross Coach Station at the end of its long journey from Scotland. These vehicles were heavily used on the London service in the first season, when increased duplication was granted for the period of the Empire Exhibition held at Battersea Park, particularly as delivery of the 20 underfloor engined vehicles was not complete until August 1951.

May, the Scottish Bus Group had also prepared a proposal which they submitted to British Railways for a Road/Rail inter-availability to be made available at extra cost (£1), giving passengers the option to travel by train on their outward or return journeys. This approach was specifically aimed at helping to counter Northern Roadways competition, though it is interesting to note that Western's minute books never made reference to any consideration being given to provide similar hostess services of food and drink on the coach service section.

Whilst Northern objected to the Scottish Bus Group's request for duplication, they also applied for both increased duplication on their London services and the addition of pick up points at Hamilton (for the Glasgow route) and Hawick (for the Edinburgh route). Permission was granted in June 1951 to operate six additional vehicles as duplicates during the period of the Empire Exhibition, (although the application for the pick up points was withdrawn in August 1951) in comparison to the Scottish Bus Group's twelve. Despite the Scottish Bus Group's concern that the granting of this increased application might jeopardize agreement by the British Transport Commission to the Road and Rail interavailability, this facility was introduced on 17th September. By December 1951, the Scottish Bus Group reported that the interavailability tickets had generated 1893 bookings on the Edinburgh/Glasgow to London services.

Four of Northern's Plaxton-bodied Maudslay Marathons were down-seated to 26 seats from 33 (although, they effectively operated as 24-seaters) and fitted retrospectively with toilets to provide additional capacity for the express services. These coaches had their own specific crews, whereas the front line fleet was driven by a pool of drivers. When these vehicles were used on the express services, to keep their operation economic (they

Timetable leaflets were produced for the London and Birmingham express services. Both promoted the 'Roadliner' name, as well as the term 'Pullman Deluxe', associating a combination of airline and railway Pullman style service. The early London leaflets featured a side profile of a coach from the 1940s. (Garry Ward Collection)

had six less seats than the Burlingham-bodied fleet), a hostess would serve her own full size coach and the Maudslay at the various stopping points. Hot drinks were supplied from the full size coach.

An additional AEC Regal IV with a Burlingham Seagull body was provided by a small independent operator, Fleming of Bannockburn. Registered DMS 676, the coach was purchased new by Fleming in 1951 and painted in full Northern livery; Jimmy Fleming provided the coach on hire to Northern until at least 1952. Some vehicle trading also took place with Fleming, four of Northern Roadways' half-cab coaches being sold to him in the early 1950s. There is also evidence of some unofficial operation of the Glasgow to London service out with the licensed service. A friend specifically recalls his family being booked on a Northern Roadways service to London using a hired coach (in 'rainbow colours') operated from John Street, on the opposite (east) side of the city centre from the normal Blytheswood Square departure point. Passengers were specifically requested to 'keep quiet' about their journey which took place in 1951/2.

Less publicity was given by the commercial press to the Glasgow to Birmingham service, which also used the Burlingham Seagull-bodied AEC Regal IVs and Leyland Royal Tigers, complete with hostess service. Buses left Blytheswood Square, Glasgow and Birmingham (Smithfield Garage) at 8pm, arriving 9:45am the following day. Fares were £2 17s 6d (£2.88p) return and a separate four page publicity leaflet in blue and red was produced, giving details of the service. In common with the Glasgow-London service, coaches picked up at Hamilton (Duke Street). Generally, their first stop and driver changeover was at Gretna, then Garstang and, finally, Whitchurch, the latter stop being near to an Airfield. Passengers were dropped off at Northern's booking agent, Browns Travel, in Erdington, near Birmingham and at the terminal point, Smithfield Garage, which was centrally located opposite the Bull Ring. However, the garage was only small and Northern coaches were normally taken back to Ken Flight's premises at Aston, where they were cleaned out, fuelled and parked up until scheduled for return to Glasgow in the evening. On Saturdays, they were often used on football hires, the key proviso being that they were returned, washed and fuelled in time for the return journey to Glasgow.

The Maudslays with toilet compartments were also operated on the Scarborough route along with the six new Bedford SBs with Duple C33F bodies purchased in 1951. This service was advertised in contemporary Northern Roadways publicity as a 'Pullman Deluxe' service. Whilst catering facilities were not offered, the benefits of a warm rug, armchair seats and wide observation windows were advertised for each passenger, plus (of course) trained drivers. The service operated daily from May to September, leaving at 9:00am from Blytheswood Square, Glasgow, with short stops at Abington for morning tea, Penrith for lunch (for one hour, scheduled to arrive at 1:44pm) and Boroughbridge for afternoon tea, arriving at Scarborough (Northway) at 8:30pm. The return service operated at the same departure time, stopping for morning tea at York, lunch at Scotch Corner and afternoon tea at Carlisle. Further attempts were made to expand this route by requesting permission in May 1951 to run up to four vehicles on the route Tuesday to Thursday and up to eight on other days. The application was refused in February 1952, probably because SOL had applied jointly with United for a new service between the two points which they were later granted, operating via Peebles, Galashiels and Jedburgh over the June to September period leaving on Fridays at 9:10pm southbound and Saturdays 11pm northbound. During the 1952 season, it appears that the Northern service was quite often operated by vehicles sub-contracted from other operators, primarily Bob McDowall of Kirkintilloch.

Statistics from *Passenger Transport* chart the growth of Northern Roadways. In 1948, 50 single-deckers were quoted; by 1949 this had risen to 65, with seven double-deckers. The latter remained quoted at seven for the next few years but the single-deck fleet is documented as being 75 in 1950 and 80 from 1951. Further new vehicles were obtained in 1951, one more Duple-bodied Bedford SB and seven Plaxton-bodied 33-seaters being purchased and used on a variety of duties, including the Scarborough express service, the Glasgow–Prestwick Airport route, some private hire work and tours. A single Plaxton-bodied Commer Avenger was also purchased, together with the Daimler CVD6s mentioned earlier and, for the contract fleet, a wartime AEC Regent and Leyland TD7, ex-Edinburgh Corporation.

NORTHERN ROADWAYS

Express PULLMAN DE LUXE Coach Service

BETWEEN

GLASGOW
AND
SCARBOROUGH

(MAY TO SEPTEMBER)

Single Fare £1 5 0   Return Fare £2 0 0

RESERVATIONS

Reservations are made only on receipt of fares and can be obtained from your Travel Agent:—

or at

The Company's General Booking Agents:

GLASGOW:
TRAVEL TRIPS LTD. - - - 22 Renfield Street

EDINBURGH:
TRAVEL TRIPS LTD. - - - 50/52 Hanover Street

HAMILTON:
TRAVEL TRIPS LTD. - - - 77/79 Cadzow Street

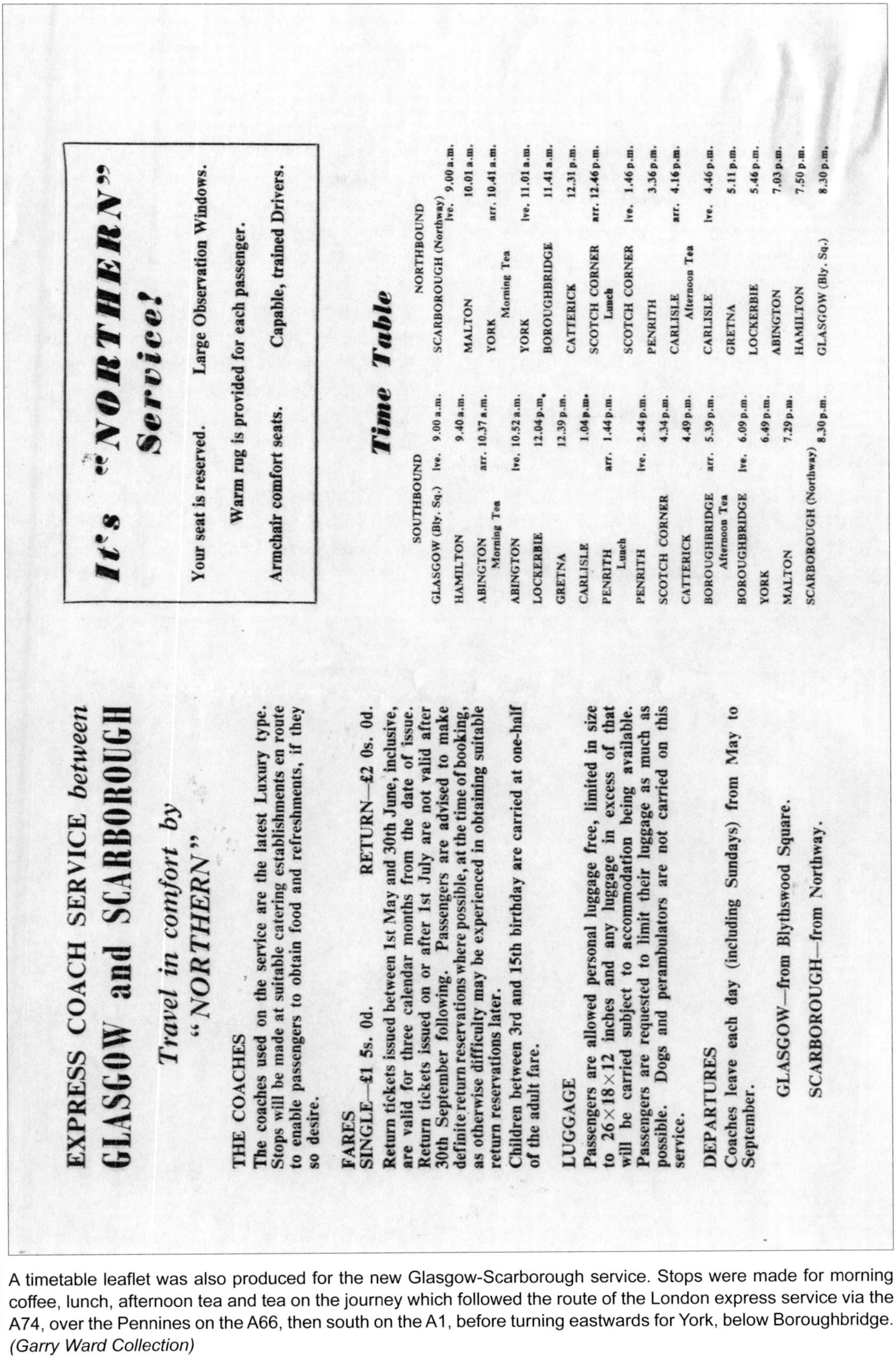

EXPRESS COACH SERVICE between
GLASGOW and SCARBOROUGH

Travel in comfort by "NORTHERN"

THE COACHES
The coaches used on the service are the latest Luxury type. Stops will be made at suitable catering establishments en route to enable passengers to obtain food and refreshments, if they so desire.

FARES
SINGLE—£1 5s. 0d.   RETURN—£2 0s. 0d.

Return tickets issued between 1st May and 30th June, inclusive, are valid for three calendar months from the date of issue. Return tickets issued on or after 1st July are not valid after 30th September following. Passengers are advised to make definite return reservations where possible, at the time of booking, as otherwise difficulty may be experienced in obtaining suitable return reservations later.

Children between 3rd and 15th birthday are carried at one-half of the adult fare.

LUGGAGE
Passengers are allowed personal luggage free, limited in size to 26×18×12 inches and any luggage in excess of that will be carried subject to accommodation being available. Passengers are requested to limit their luggage as much as possible. Dogs and perambulators are not carried on this service.

DEPARTURES
Coaches leave each day (including Sundays) from May to September.

GLASGOW—from Blythswood Square.

SCARBOROUGH—from Northway.

It's "NORTHERN" Service!

Your seat is reserved.   Large Observation Windows.

Warm rug is provided for each passenger.

Armchair comfort seats.   Capable, trained Drivers.

Time Table

SOUTHBOUND

GLASGOW (Bly. Sq.)	lve.	9.00 a.m.
HAMILTON		9.40 a.m.
ABINGTON	arr.	10.37 a.m.
Morning Tea		
ABINGTON	lve.	10.52 a.m.
LOCKERBIE		12.04 p.m.
GRETNA		12.39 p.m.
CARLISLE		1.04 p.m.
PENRITH	arr.	1.44 p.m.
Lunch		
PENRITH	lve.	2.44 p.m.
SCOTCH CORNER		4.34 p.m.
CATTERICK		4.49 p.m.
BOROUGHBRIDGE	arr.	5.39 p.m.
Afternoon Tea		
BOROUGHBRIDGE	lve.	6.09 p.m.
YORK		6.49 p.m.
MALTON		7.29 p.m.
SCARBOROUGH (Northway)		8.30 p.m.

NORTHBOUND

SCARBOROUGH (Northway)	lve.	9.00 a.m.
MALTON		10.01 a.m.
YORK	arr.	10.41 a.m.
Morning Tea		
YORK	lve.	11.01 a.m.
BOROUGHBRIDGE		11.41 a.m.
CATTERICK		12.31 p.m.
SCOTCH CORNER	arr.	12.46 p.m.
Lunch		
SCOTCH CORNER	lve.	1.46 p.m.
PENRITH		3.36 p.m.
CARLISLE	arr.	4.16 p.m.
Afternoon Tea		
CARLISLE	lve.	4.46 p.m.
GRETNA		5.11 p.m.
LOCKERBIE		5.46 p.m.
ABINGTON		7.03 p.m.
HAMILTON		7.50 p.m.
GLASGOW (Bly. Sq.)		8.30 p.m.

A timetable leaflet was also produced for the new Glasgow-Scarborough service. Stops were made for morning coffee, lunch, afternoon tea and tea on the journey which followed the route of the London express service via the A74, over the Pennines on the A66, then south on the A1, before turning eastwards for York, below Boroughbridge. *(Garry Ward Collection)*

Subsequent to the use of the garage near Eglington Toll, Northern moved into premises at the Meat Market in Gallowgate, on the east side of the city. The building was, apparently, too big for use by the market, with the result that one of the sections, which was roofed but open sided, was leased out for use by Northern Roadways. Later, the premises were used by another Glasgow independent, Cotters of Glasgow, mentioned earlier. A large yard was also occupied in Hyndland, north of the Clyde on the west side of the City, off Clarence Drive at the junction of Lauderdale Gardens and Turnberry Road.

Some covered accommodation was also available within the yard, although only suitable for single-deckers. Three vehicles at a time could be maintained in the shed, but the premises were noted as lacking pits, a ramp or adequate lighting, and jacks were relied on to provide access underneath buses. A fourth vehicle was sometimes squeezed into the entrance, which was only some eighteen inches higher than height of standard single-deckers, where partial coverage could be provided to allow work to be undertaken.

However, the rapid expansion of the early 'fifties and the need to support an express service operation drove the need for better equipped premises. Plans were passed for a new garage and workshops at Helen Street, Govan, this time south of the Clyde although still in the west of the city, which would, it was claimed, be capable of housing a fleet of over 100 vehicles. The new garage was built and occupied during 1951 and provided facilities, amongst other things, for the storage of pillows and rugs, fuelling of coaches, a wash bay and toilet cleaning section and a suspended water feeder for filling the coach boilers. The express coach fleet, together with the tour and private hire coaches were moved into Helen Street. However, the old premises at Hyndland were

The new batch of Bedford SBs, Northern's first forward-control Bedfords, were used on the Scarborough service. SMU 960 was one of six purchased in 1951 with Duple 33-seat coach bodies and is pictured here at Prestwick Airport, probably on a day tour from Glasgow. It carries the Northern scroll fleet name transfer on the side, whilst other vehicles had raised metal fleet name plates. The batch carried mixed registrations, the others being JGB 948-9 and WMT 337, 567 and 568. *(Garry Ward Collection)*

A 'one off' new Commer Avenger with Plaxton 33-seat coachwork was also purchased in 1951. JGD 546 is in central London on a tour. It carries a chromium plated Northern fleet name on its side panel. One further Duple bodied Bedford SB, together with seven Plaxton-bodied Bedford SB's were delivered in 1951/2.

The rapid expansion of the fleet and the introduction of express services made the move to a new garage with suitable facilities, from premises at the Meat Market in Gallowgate and the Hyndland yard more urgent. The new Helen Street premises in Govan were occupied during 1951 and nine of the Burlingham Seagull-bodied express coaches are seen inside the garage, between duties. The filling caps for the boiler can just be seen towards the rear of each coach on the offside; they were filled from a hose linked to a gantry within the garage. *(Robert Grieves Collection)*

The garage provided maintenance facilities for the fleet and AEC Regal JGE 422 is receiving attention over the pit. According to a Commercial Motor feature at the time, drivers were encouraged to follow up on problems with vehicles as well as report them for action by the fitters. Most, if not all, of the fleet of express coaches appear to have originally been delivered with single headlights and were later fitted, like JGE 422, with additional lights within the first year of operation. *(Robert Grieves Collection)*

As well as pits, the garage was equipped with a hoist and AEC Regal IV, JGD 117 is receiving attention from two of the engineering staff. The 'Sun Rise' obscured leaded light glass extended around the toilet compartment and cupboard storage area immediately aft of it on the offside; the near side rear most window was glazed in clear glass. Over a period of time, the semaphore indicators fitted towards the front were panelled over; they were prone to sticking and provided little indication to following traffic which way a vehicle was turning. *(Robert Grieves Collection)*

also retained and, later, provided the original base for much of the contract fleet used on school services. It is known that the large fleet of ex-Birmingham Daimlers and Leyland Titans purchased in 1954 operated from this base for a time.

Further battles and consolidation

Further express service expansion was planned by Northern Roadways, when they applied in October 1951 for new express services between Glasgow (Blytheswood Square) and Bournemouth (Keystone Garage) and between Edinburgh (Queen Street) and Bournemouth, operating April to October, picking up and setting down at both points plus Southampton (Grosvenor Square Garage), with fares of £3 single and £4 12s 6d return. They also applied for new express services from both Glasgow and Edinburgh to Dover (Priory Hotel), picking up and setting down at both points plus Folkestone (Marine Parade Coach Park), operating April to October, leaving Glasgow or Edinburgh at 1:30pm and returning from Dover at 7:30pm (fares £3 single and £4 15s 0d return). The Northern application for the Dover services followed similar applications some ten months earlier by Sibbald Roadways as mentioned earlier.

Northern applied to operate these express services around the weekend time frame, except during the period 1st June to 30th September, when they wished to operate daily. These applications were slightly revised in the 20th October submission to limit picking up and setting down to those passengers whose journeys originated in Scotland. Not surprisingly, a large number of objections were raised to all of these applications by Western SMT, SOL (for Edinburgh based services), the Railway Executive, Yelloway, Standerwick, Ribble, Alexanders, David Lawson, Cotters, Lowland Motorways, BMMO, Western National (for Bournemouth services) and Associated Motorways, plus East Kent Road Car additionally for Dover services. The hearings were set for 5th–7th February 1952.

Despite the number of objectors, the Glasgow to Bournemouth service was granted for the period June to September, uplifting and setting down in Glasgow and Bournemouth only with return tickets only being issued at a fare of £4 (inclusive of refreshments) to leave Glasgow on Fridays and Saturdays at 6pm and Bournemouth on Saturdays and Sundays at 6pm. The Edinburgh to Bournemouth application was withdrawn. The Bournemouth service was a real marathon scheduled to take 18 hours and 35 minutes, arriving at 12:35pm the next day, one of the longest express journeys in the country at that time.

The service started on 5th June 1952 and operated via Hamilton, Abington, Lockerbie, Carlisle, Kendal, Lancaster, Newcastle-Under-Lyme, Lichfield, Warwick, Banbury, Oxford, Newbury, Winchester and Southampton. In the early days, the Scottish crew of two drivers took the vehicle as far as Banbury where a locally-based driver would take the coach onward to Bournemouth and return with it the same night. Stops en-route on the Bournemouth service were at the discretion of the drivers and depended on traffic conditions. It appears that the use of a Banbury-based driver was by no means the norm and, often, the two drivers would take the coach all the way to Bournemouth. In times of heavy traffic the service could take as much as 21 hours. No accommodation was provided for the drivers or stewardess, as there was so little time before the return journey. If they were on schedule, the crew would have around five hours to clean out the coach, grab some sleep and prepare for the return journey north, leaving at 6pm the same day. Jimmy Connor recalls that they sometimes walked along the beach to get some fresh air. No refuelling or washing of the coach was carried out at this terminal point, which was centrally placed near the Promenade.

The service provided a valuable direct (and comfortable) connection for holidaymakers wishing to travel to Bournemouth, without the need to make changes. Alternatives were the more expensive train journey or via the 'Westlinks' coach connections provided through the Associated Motorways hub at Cheltenham. The latter involved an even longer 22 hour marathon journey, passengers using the 10pm Glasgow to Liverpool service, operated jointly by Ribble and Western SMT, then changing to the Ribble express service to Cheltenham the following day, connecting into one of the 2pm departures from the Associated Motorways Coach Station at Cheltenham. Passengers finally arrived at

Bournemouth at 8pm, having made two changes and travelled on 'ordinary' coaches. They also paid £4 4s 0d, four shillings more than the direct competing service, with hostess service, operated by Northern Roadways.

Further applications were made in January 1952 for a new tour from Blytheswood Square, Glasgow to Prestwick Airport, including a sightseeing tour, using a maximum of 12 vehicles, running May to September. The licence was granted in July 1952, allowing one vehicle during the week and two at weekends and public holidays. Additionally, new tours based on the Ben Wyvis Hotel, Strathpeffer were applied for from Blytheswood Square, Glasgow and Queen Street, Edinburgh, April to October on Saturdays only.

The battle on the London road continued, with applications by both Western SMT and SMT in February 1952 to run up to 26 vehicles daily in the period 1st June to 30th September (*ie* the same levels operated in 1951 during the Exhibition) on their services from Glasgow and Edinburgh to London. The application was prompted by, to quote the Western SMT minute books of the time, receipt of 'specific information'.

An apparently fatal blow was dealt to Northern's express services when, in March 1952, the Minister of Transport, JS Maclay, announced his decision on the Scottish Bus Group and Railway Executive's appeal to the granting of the licences (presumably the 'specific information' mentioned above). All except the Bridlington services, which operated, effectively, as seven day tours from Edinburgh and Glasgow, were to be cancelled. On the revocation of their express licences, Northern Roadways appealed in April 1952 to continue until September pending a formal appeal, as they held 33,000 single journey bookings over the period and wished to be able to satisfy these. The April 1952 Notices and Proceedings confirmed that the appeal to continue until the end of September was granted.

That is not to say that the Scottish Bus Group got things all their own way. They had repeatedly voiced concerns regarding the danger of other operators viewing Northern's previous success as a reason for them applying for new services and removals of restrictions to existing routes. They had appealed against the granting of additional vehicles to operate for Neil Beaton of Portree on the island of Skye on their service from Glasgow (Bath Hotel) to Portree and the appeal was reported

to have been refused in March 1952.

A number of operators (some established and some new) had also been making applications for new services, with mixed results. A company called Highland Transport of Penilee, Glasgow applied for a series of express services during 1951 and 1952. Their first application was made before Northern Roadways commenced their London services when, in January 1951, Highland Transport applied for a service from Glasgow (Washington Street) to Corby via Motherwell, Wishaw, Lanark, Lockerbie, Penrith, Scotch Corner and Grantham. The service was to operate on Friday evenings from Glasgow, returning from Corby on Sundays and was designed to cater for the large population of workers who had migrated from the Central Scottish belt to the steel works which had been established in the Midlands town.

A similar application was made in May 1951 from the other end of the proposed route by Thistle Services (Benefield) Ltd, based in Oundle near Peterborough. Their application was more specific 'to accommodate the large number of Scottish workers at Stewarts & Lloyds Steel works and to provide relatives with a means of visiting these workers'. Despite objections from Western SMT and the Railway executive, this application, inclusive of backing licences, succeeded in June 1951. Also successful was a subsequent application to include Leicester, Loughborough and Nottingham as pick up and drop-off points. The service, which terminated at Parkhead Cross in the east end of Glasgow, was subsequently acquired by Barton of Chilwell (jointly with Robin Hood Coaches) in November 1954.

Highland Transport's earlier Corby service application failed, as did an application made in December 1950 for a Glasgow to Southampton service (following a similar route to the later Northern Roadways service to Bournemouth), but they persisted with further applications in June 1951 for services from Glasgow (St Enoch Square) and Edinburgh to the large army base at Catterick Camp near Richmond in North Yorkshire, to operate southbound on Fridays and Sundays and return on Saturdays and Mondays. Although the application was withdrawn in December 1951, it triggered applications for alternative excursions and tours licences from Catterick Camp to Glasgow and Edinburgh by many local operators in the area over the next year or so, including

Scotts Greys of Darlington and Beeline Roadways of West Hartlepool, all of which the Scottish Bus Group and others successfully opposed. Highland made a further fresh application for a Glasgow to Southampton service in July 1951 together with a new application for a Glasgow to Coventry service, extending beyond the Birmingham terminal point of the Northern Roadways service. Both these applications were also refused in April 1952. Highland Transports' final attempt was an application in September 1951 for a service from Glasgow (St Enoch Square) to Scrabster to provide connections with the ferry service to the Orkney Isles, operating May to September, Friday, Sunday and Tuesday northbound and Saturday, Monday and Wednesday southbound. This application was also refused in April 1952, although Highland lodged an appeal, subsequently refused by the Minister of Transport in November 1952. This appears to have ended their interest in express coach services.

The established operator R Dickson of Dundee also entered the fray, applying in March 1951 for an express service from the Aberdeen tour stance to London (Victoria) via Stonehaven, Arbroath, Dundee, Perth, Stirling, Lanark, Lockerbie, Penrith and Scotch Corner during May to September. This application was later withdrawn, probably due to the level of objections.

Another entrepreneur with plans to expand into coaching and express services was George Rodger of Motherwell, who had been a haulage contractor and had sold his business shortly after World War 2. He is believed to have had 'connections' with Northern Roadways and progressed as far as ordering twelve new Leyland Royal Tigers with Leyland coach bodies, although no formal applications for services had been progressed in his name. When his plans did not come to fruition the cancelled order was transferred to W Alexander, who took ten of the batch in 1952 with the other two passing to Hutchison of Overtown.

At that time, the commercial press reported that Northern's vehicles were employed thus during the summer; eight on the Scotland-London service, four on the Glasgow-Scarborough and six on the Glasgow-Birmingham. The latter service had carried 17,000 passengers by the end of 1952. Disputes were reported to have arisen on the London services as a result of Northern Roadways inadvertently running more vehicles than they were licensed to do so on the backing licence of the London services from the Metropolitan

Traffic Area, with four coaches being operated on each service instead of two. Northern insisted that this mistake happened on a few Sundays.

No time was lost in attempting to maximize the remaining operations on the Summer 1952 services; applications were made for duplication of their Glasgow and Edinburgh to London services to run up to 20 vehicles in each direction (both refused 17th May 1952) and Glasgow to Scarborough to run up to 10 vehicles (for the latter service on Friday, Saturday, Sunday and Monday). The London services actually had a partial grant of increased duplication of four vehicles per day on the London services by the Scottish Traffic Authority but backing was not forthcoming from the Metropolitan and the Scarborough duplication application was withdrawn in June 1952.

Northern Roadways also promptly re-applied for the licences revoked as follows on 3rd May 1952;

Glasgow (West section of West George Street) and Scarborough (Northway) to operate daily May to September, leaving Glasgow and Scarborough at 9am, with not more than four vehicles Tuesday to Thursday and not more than 20 vehicles Friday to Monday.

Glasgow (West section of West George Street) and Birmingham (Smithfield Garage, Digbeth) to operate daily, leaving Glasgow and Birmingham at 8pm with not more than three vehicles November to April and not more than six, May to October.

Glasgow (West section of West George Street) and London (Kings Cross Coach Station) to operate daily leaving Glasgow at 6:30pm and London at 7:30pm with not more than ten vehicles May to October and Christmas to New Year, with four in the period November to April.

Edinburgh (Queen Street) and London (Kings Cross Coach Station) to operate daily leaving Edinburgh at 6:30pm and London at 7:30pm with not more than ten vehicles May to October and Christmas to New Year, with four in the period November to April.

A 'new' licence was also applied for at the same time between Glasgow St Enoch Hotel and Prestwick Airport for airline passengers and friends and persons using the Airport in connection with Trans Canada Airlines, Pan American and SAS, daily to suit airline schedules and taking up and setting down at both terminal points only. Short term licences were granted for operation during May and June 1952. Also in June, further expansion was planned when an application was made for new nine

This photograph and the following one shows a representative selection of the fleet outside the Helen Street Garage in 1952. Left to right are JGD 113, one of the 'front line' express service AEC Regal IV's with Burlingham body, GGB 362, the Scottish Aviation bodied Crossley which, by then, had been joined by three similar examples (ASN 348, 587 and 588) acquired with the licences of Clydebank Co-operative's coaching arm, AMS 328 an ex-Alexander Bedford OWB illustrated earlier and GGE 842, one of the Barnard bodied Daimler CVD6s purchased new. *(Robert Grieves Collection)*

day tours from Glasgow and Edinburgh to Ramsgate, operating on Saturdays from May to September. In November 1952, the full express service licence to Prestwick Airport operated for Pan American Airways and Trans Canada Airlines was granted.

Despite the major concerns over the impending extinguishing of most of the express licences, the summer of 1952 was probably the high point of Northern Roadways operation. At that time, they had express services to London from both Edinburgh and Glasgow, a Glasgow to Birmingham express service, seasonal express services from Glasgow to Bournemouth and Glasgow to Scarborough and a seven day tours licence from both Glasgow and Edinburgh to Bridlington. Additionally, they had tours licences from both Glasgow and Edinburgh to Strathpeffer in connection with their associated Ben Wyvis Hotel, a tours licence from Glasgow to Colintraive, the excursions and tours business taken over from Clydebank Cooperative Society operating from Alexander Street, Clydebank, plus services from Glasgow to Prestwick Airport, contract operations in Glasgow and Beith, the latter primarily centered

on the RNAD services, an important private hire business, plus a growing Northern Ayrshire Coaches subsidiary with services in the Irvine and Kilwinning area and applications pending for new express services from both Glasgow and Edinburgh to Dover and a new tours licence from both Glasgow and Edinburgh to Ramsgate. Additionally, they had ordered a new coach for operation on the express services. Commercial press details of the time promised new restyled vehicles, based on operating experience and airline practice studied.

The associated travel agency, Travel Trips Ltd had four offices by then; the head office by 1952 was quoted as 20 Renfield Street, Glasgow (moving to 45 Renfield Street by 1961), 23 Princes Street, Edinburgh (shortly to move to 50/2 Hanover Street, Edinburgh), 41 Causeyside Street, Paisley and, finally, 77-9 Cadzow Street, Hamilton. Harry McGhee's brother, Jack McGhee, sometimes called J Anderson McGhee was in charge of the Continental travel and air travel booking at Travel Trips, as well as having a hand in producing the travel brochures. A quality illustrated tours booklet entitled 'The Silent Courier' was produced for

The second photograph, which is likely to have been taken at the same time, shows GUS 292, a Plaxton bodied Maudslay Marathon III, JUS 493, one of the seven Plaxton-bodied Bedford SBs purchased in 1951/2 (the others being JGD 669-671, JUS 491-2 and JYS 453) and GUS 816, another of the Plaxton-bodied Maudslays converted to 26-seater coaches with toilets. *(Robert Grieves Collection)*

"The Silent Courier"

Detailed & Illustrated Itineraries
OF THE
STRATHPEFFER TOURS

Souvenir Copy presented to

_____

With the Compliments of

TRAVEL TRIPS LIMITED · GLASGOW · EDINBURGH · AND BRANCH

GLASGOW DEPARTURES

The front cover of 'The Silent Courier', a tours booklet, in this case for the Strathpeffer tours produced in the early 'fifties, which was presented to each passenger carried on one of Northern Roadways' tours. *(Garry Ward Collection)*

Index

THE BEN WYVIS HOTEL, STRATHPEFFER SPA, ROSS-SHIRE—YOUR HOME DURING THE TOUR

This Strathpeffer Tours booklet included an illustration of the Ben Wyvis Hotel, from which day tours would be based, along with three Maudslay coaches and their occupants, posed for the camera. Travel Trips and Northern Roadways staff would help out at the hotel from time to time. *(Garry Ward Collection)*

A map of the Strathpeffer 7 day tour, taken from a tours booklet produced in the early 'fifties. The day tours operated as a 'fantail', based on the Ben Wyvis Hotel and a detailed description of each day's route, attractions and landmarks was provided, together with supporting illustrations, one of which showed three Bedford OBs close to Dornoch Firth. *(Garry Ward Collection)*

passengers on the Strathpeffer tours based at the associated Ben Wyvis Hotel. The book was intended to supplement the commentary given by the driver and gave detailed itineraries for the tours. The Strathpeffer tours tended to have regular drivers including one who also acted as chauffeur for Harry McGhee.

For a period, Northern Roadways also provided the team coaches for both Rangers and Celtic. The express coaches were used on a number of occasions for prestigious hires. For example, two London coaches were diverted to pick up the Los Praegor orchestra, which had been playing at the London Palladium and were scheduled to appear in Glasgow. It is understood that Northern also hired out coaches to MacBraynes periodically in the early 'fifties.

Returning to the licence applications, the Edinburgh and Glasgow to Dover applications were withdrawn on 12th July 1952, a commercial passenger transport publication of the time quoting the reason as being the degree of opposition to the services. However, it is more than likely that Northern needed to concentrate their efforts on appealing for the reinstatement of the existing express services before they were due to cease. The results of those efforts were made known in October and November 1952.

A primary licence for the Glasgow to Birmingham service was granted on 1st November, with the restrictions that in the period May to September not more than three vehicles could be operated from each terminus and between October and April not more than two vehicles could be operated. The service was restricted to passengers travelling from Glasgow, despite further appeals from Northern Roadways. However, this restriction was later lifted as we shall see.

New primary licences were granted for the Glasgow to London service on 4th July 1952 as follows; 1st October to 30th April not more than six vehicles allowed to operate with not more than four from one terminus. From 16th December to 15th January not more than eight vehicles allowed to operate with not more than six from one terminus. Glasgow Spring holiday Friday to Monday not more than eight vehicles allowed to operate with not more than six from one terminus. 1st May to 30th September Friday, Saturday, Sunday and Monday not more than eight vehicles allowed to operate with not more than six from one terminus. Tuesday, Wednesday and Thursday not more than six vehicles to operate with not more than four from one terminus.

The Edinburgh to London service also had a primary licence granted on the same day as follows; 1st October to 30th April not more than four vehicles allowed to operate with not more than three from one terminus. From 16th December to 15th January not more than six vehicles allowed to operate with not more than four from one terminus. 1st May to 30th September, six vehicles to operate with not more than four from one terminus. In November, the Metropolitan Authority granted reduced backing licences of two vehicles in any direction for both Edinburgh and Glasgow to London services, having deferred the decision from October.

The protracted hearings illustrated that the objectors did not see Northern as supplying a service any different from that which they provided, whilst Northern's own witnesses condemned the service given by their competitors. Much publicity surrounded this battle and there was considerable support and sympathy for Northern's plight. Northern were assisted by the considerable number of testimonial letters which they had received, praising the service, the facilities and the staff. The Scottish Bus Group reacted immediately, not surprisingly, by lodging an appeal.

Two months later, in December, the Ramsgate licence was granted. The Ramsgate excursion and tours licence operated in a similar manner to the Strathpeffer tours. Northern Roadways had purchased the 118 room Regency Hotel in Ramsgate early in 1952 and appointed a manager who had previously been based in Rothesay to run it. After an official opening which both local signatories and company senior management attended, the hotel opened for business. At the time of the hotel purchase, it had been intended that a new company would be formed to operate it and in December 1952 Regency Hotel (Ramsgate) Ltd was incorporated to take over the assets. Appeals were also lodged by the Scottish Bus Group against this licence as well as the Bournemouth express services.

Notwithstanding these victories in the Traffic Courts, the first retraction was witnessed when the Glasgow to Scarborough application was withdrawn in 29th November 1952 having operated for just two seasons, thus abandoning this route. By then SOL, jointly with United Automobile Services, had built up a comprehensive service from both Glasgow and Edinburgh to the coastal resort, including a summer-only overnight service mentioned earlier.

In addition, the Northern Ayrshire Coaches subsidiary was advertised for sale, including eleven vehicles and three stage carriage routes. One of their principal rivals in Ayrshire, the AA Co-operative trading as AA Motor Services Ltd., expressed an interest. The Kilbirnie and Beith area of Northern's Ayrshire Coaches operations was also put up for sale, these licences being held by parent Northern Roadways, although operated by Northern Ayrshire. Northern Ayrshire's initial fleet had been made up of vehicles acquired with Walker, Kilbirnie and one vehicle from Hicks. These had been augmented and, in some cases, replaced by a combination of vehicles from the parent company, Bedford OBs and Maudslay Marathons, plus second-hand purchases of pre-war Leyland Tigers from Chesterfield Corporation.

On the positive side, in the same month, a new coach was unveiled at the Commercial Motor Show for use on the express services. Built on the relatively uncommon Daimler 'Freeline' chassis, the coach had been fitted with a Duple Ambassador body of considerable luxury. Finished in the usual silver and blue livery, the coach had glazed roof panels, a tartan waistband, the two 'Glengarrys' and a chrome 'Northern Roadways' fleet name on either side. Internally, reclining seats for 30 passengers, a toilet compartment and storage cupboards were fitted.

The coach became the pride of the fleet (often referred to as the Coronation coach) and there were brave words from Northern of this vehicle being the precursor to a batch of new vehicles. In the event, it remained unique. Its first job was to transport officials of the Clyde Football Club to Wembley to the Scotland-England match.

The express services settled down to a short period of relative calm, interrupted by applications by rivals SOL and Western SMT for an increase in the vehicles operated over the Coronation period of 50 more vehicles from both Glasgow and Edinburgh to London between 24th May and 14th June. The Scottish Traffic Commissioners granted an interim increase to a maximum of 26 a day over the period from 24th May to 31st May and a maximum of 34 vehicles per day over the period 1st June to 14th June, until British Railways own arrangements were known in December 1952.

Northern unveiled a new express coach at the 1952 Commercial Motor Show, built on Daimler's answer to the underfloor engined models of other manufacturers, the Freeline, which was to remain generally uncommon and, in Northern's case, unique, fitted with a Duple Ambassador body, this time with seating for only 30. Like the Burlingham-bodied coaches LGA 405 was fitted with a toilet, storage areas for cups etc and a boiler for providing hot drinks. Its appearance at the Show gave many professional bus men their first opportunity to review the type of coach and facilities provided by Northern Roadways and some voiced their opinion that it was 'over providing' for the public. *(Ian Maclean Collection)*

LGA 405 entered service in April 1953 and became 'Pride of the Fleet', being hired for prestigious work, as well as being used on the express services. There was talk of the vehicle being the first of a new fleet, but it remained unique; in fact, it was actually the last underfloor engined coach purchased! It was the only coach to carry the full Northern Roadways fleet name on the side, carried on chrome finish letters, together with the' NR" initials carried within further chrome embellishments towards the rear. The coach is loading passengers for London at Blytheswood Square with AEC Regal IV coach JGD 116. *(Ian Maclean Collection)*

LGA 405 at King's Cross Coach station in the company of another Northern coach. One of Birch Brothers Birch-bodied Leyland PD1s can just be seen to the extreme left. Northern specified glazed roof panels on the 'Coronation Coach', as it was christened, which were more common for touring coaches rather than express vehicles. With centre entrances, which were common in the new era of under floor engined coaches at that time, the nearside front seats next to the driver were much sought after. In practice, these were often occupied by the second driver and the hostess when the coaches were quieter.

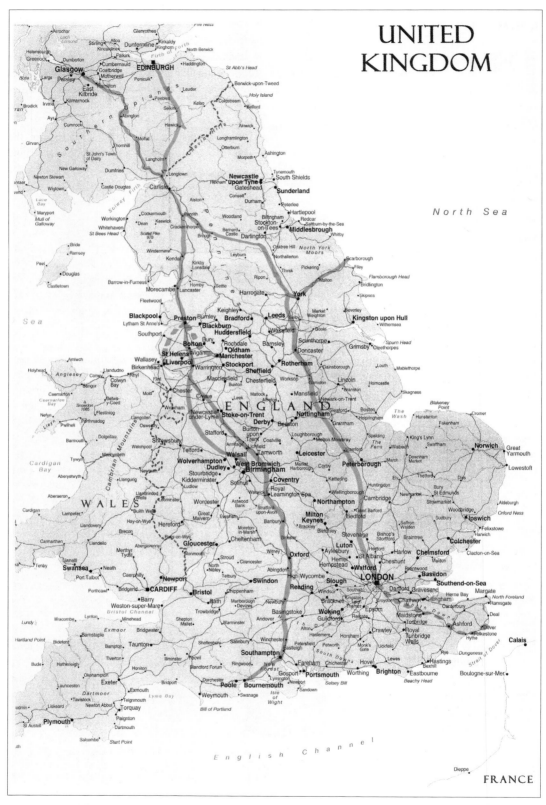

Map showing the extent of Northern Roadways express services and proposed express services.

Contraction in Ayrshire

Discussions around the possible sale of the Irvine area operations of Northern Ayrshire Coaches Ltd to AA Motor Services were initiated early in 1953. Northern were keen to sell both the services and a number of vehicles but AA Motor Services, initially, were only prepared to make an offer for the goodwill of the licences held.

In the event, the Kilbirnie and Beith area segment of Northern Ayrshire's operations was sold first, passing to a newly formed company, Garnock Valley Coaches of Kilbirnie, together with six assorted vehicles (a Daimler CVD6 from the parent Northern fleet and Bedford OWB ASD 305, two Bedford OBs BES 790 and BES 973 and two Leyland TS7cs CRA 264/5 from Northern Ayrshire Coaches). The licences transferred (which were held in Northern Roadways name), covered the Kilbirnie (Lynn Drive) and Beith (Auldlea Road) service, Lochwinnoch to Beith (Spiers School) and tours licences. However, the Beith RNAD services remained with Northern at that time.

AA's negotiations with Northern on the Irvine area operations were a protracted affair. Their original offer of £5,000 for the goodwill of the services was rejected in June, but a month later, a takeover figure of £9,500 was agreed the Irvine area services, plus five vehicles; two Leyland TS8s (ERA 90 and 91), two Maudslays (GGA 565 and 656) and a Bedford OB (BGS 536). AA proposed to take over the services on 15th August 1953, with vehicles operating on hire to Northern Ayrshire Coaches Ltd until the licences were transferred, effectively ending the very short existence of the latter company in a little over four years. The AA directors agreed to share out the vehicles by drawing lots. The vehicles were allocated as follows: Dodds, 1948 Maudslay GGA 656; Law, 1948 Maudslay GGA 565; Tumilty, 1937 Leyland ERA 90; Young, 1937 Leyland ERA 91. The Bedford OB was not wanted by any of the AA partners and it was offered back to Napier of Northern, who had initially expressed an interest in acquiring the vehicle, but this came to nothing. It was retained by AA until its eventual sale in February 1954 to SMT Sales and Service. An additional Northern Roadways vehicle was added by AA partner, Dodds, when one of the Burlingham-bodied AEC Regal IV coaches was acquired via Millburn Motors.

The staff were re-employed between the partners and the leased garage in Fullerton Street, Irvine was put into use as a base for the local Irvine services and continued in use until at least October 1954. The Bell punch Ultimate ticket machines used were also transferred, being deemed more suitable than the Setrights for local use.

Applications were made to take over the following services; the services between Irvine (Clark Drive) and Kilwinning (Druid Drive, the service having been extended in August 1953 by Northern from Eraidwood Avenue), Irvine (Rubie Crescent) and Livingstone Terrace, Irvine (Clark Drive) and Royal Ordnance Factory in Irvine and the express service between Irvine Cross and Georgetown RAOC Factory. The Georgetown service contract was the subject of further correspondence; AA were unwilling to accept responsibility for breakdowns or late arrivals or the requirement to reimburse wages lost, as had been requested by the Camp Commander. AA did, however, agree to continue with a school service which had previously been operated by Northern Ayrshire to and from Winton Road for mornings and lunchtimes for around 70 pupils of Loudon-Montgomery Public school. The service had not been licensed and a relief vehicle was used until the services were reorganised after takeover.

AA had also received a letter from A1 Service objecting to AA taking over the services of Northern Ayrshire Coaches until some assurance was given that the fares would be co-ordinated with through services. After discussion, it was agreed to leave the A1 objection and have it brought out in the Licensing Court.

The question of alterations to the Irvine local services was discussed at length by AA in September 1953. It was agreed that although the Town Council had requested that buses come off Winton Road, it would be a retrograde step to do this as the circle was one of the main points of the scheme. If the buses followed the trunk roads of Caldon Road and Livingstone Terrace, the perimeter of the scheme would only be tapped and there would be a loss in traffic. It was finally agreed that various suggestions should be put to the Town Council and the final decision would rest with them. Included in any new proposals would be the introduction of a service to either Stewart Drive or to a point near the entrance, as there were concerns that Western SMT would push for a licence to operate from this area. Further developments were not pursued until the licences were formally transferred to AA Motor Services.

Although the sale of the Northern Ayrshire Coaches operation was the main focus, Northern also abandoned an irregular non-licensed service from Glasgow St Enoch Square to Uplawmoor (Caldwell House), with Western SMT formally applying for a licence in February 1953.

Express and Military contract consolidation

Active competition remained in most aspects of Northern's services. Western applied for a new tour from Glasgow Cunningham Street to Prestwick Airport, countering Northern Roadways tour licence, to operate May to September with a maximum of 12 vehicles. Northern Roadways objected, but the licence was granted on 27th December 1952, restricted to one vehicle Monday to Friday and two at weekends and Glasgow Public Holidays.

Some of the uncertainty around the continued operation of the express services was removed, when it was announced in May 1953 that the Scottish Bus Group's appeal against the granting of Northern's London licences was refused. The Group were ordered to pay costs, followed the next month by the refusal of their appeals against Northern's Birmingham, Bournemouth and Ramsgate services and tours, again with the Scottish Bus Group ordered to pay costs. Thus ended two and a half years of protracted wrangling over the licence applications since Northern first made applications to run these express services. As has been said above, the whole case attracted considerable publicity, questions even being asked in the House of Commons, where it had been stated in March 1953 that there had been 14 appeals against the re-granting of the London express service licences and 16 appeals against the Birmingham express service licence. The Ministry of Transport Inspectors report on the appeal (accepted by the Minister of Transport) was that the appeals should be dismissed, based on the view that where additional facilities were found to be needed, the Road Traffic Act did not prevent licensing authorities from giving a share to a new operator. Interestingly, the Inspector did not place

any importance on the type of service provided by Northern, with hostesses, food provided and toilet facilities, the only consideration being that it was an express service.

Letters had also been flying between The British Road Federation and the British Transport Commission around remarks made by the Railway Executive during the appeal against the granting of the Birmingham express licence that the public should never have been given the opportunity to know whether they wanted the service or not. The British Road Federation was concerned that this was a policy; in reality, the remarks had been taken out of context, the Railway Executive meaning that a new licence should never have been granted given the previous revocation by the Minister of Transport. The West Midlands Traffic Area had granted a backing licence for the new application on the basis that the Scottish Traffic Area had found a need for further facilities between Glasgow and Birmingham, but retained the restriction that only return passengers from Glasgow could be carried as mentioned earlier. They had also commented that they thought the facilities provided by the Railway Executive were adequate for the amount of traffic.

Even Northern's seemingly less-controversial Ramsgate licence received coverage in the commercial press, the representative for Scottish Omnibuses Ltd describing it as two men owning a hotel in Ramsgate and a fleet of coaches in Glasgow and attempting to link the two assets by providing tours from Scotland to and from the hotel, then day tours from the hotel. It was stated to be an attempt to drive 'a cart and four' through the Road Traffic Act by focussing on the type of holiday offered rather than the transport need.

Northern gained a further concession from the Minister of Transport when he announced his decision in May 1953. Overturning the West Midlands Traffic Area condition, the Minister granted permission for passengers to be carried with single tickets from Birmingham to Glasgow, allowing 'two way traffic'. Always looking to maximize publicity for the service, Northern placed a coach on waste ground close to the centre of Birmingham for a week, staffed by drivers and hostess who had come off the Glasgow service that morning, to promote it. Midland Red were very annoyed by this action and threatened legal action on the basis that Northern had to drive the coach across a public pavement to reach the waste ground.

With the successful refusal of the appeals, Harry McGhee placed a public acknowledgement in 'The Star' newspaper in May 1953, thanking the public for their support for 'improved long distance coach services'.

Nevertheless, the Scottish Bus Group gained the 'upper hand' on the London express services, obtaining increased duplication allowances in the Coronation Year after a high profile campaign by James Amos, the Scottish Bus Group Chairman, who pushed for removal of the restrictions which, up to that point, British Railways had been able to successfully defend on the number of coaches operating to London. In turn, this resulted in Western SMT and SMT purchasing further new coaches for the London services, Western also down-seating a couple of existing Guy UF toilet coaches and fitting them out for use on their service.

Northern's contract services to military establishments were reduced further, firstly with the take over of their services from both Johnstone and Glasgow to Georgetown in December 1953, by Garners Bus Service (Bridge of Weir) Ltd. Garners already had services from both Paisley and Johnstone to Georgetown (having successfully countered Northern's Paisley applications a few years earlier) and operated a range of contract and school services, as mentioned earlier, together with a couple of stage carriage routes between Johnstone and Houston and between their home village of Bridge of Weir and Paisley over the 'Paisley Back Road' via Georgetown. No Northern vehicles passed to Garners. Additionally, some ten months after the other operations in the area were sold, Northern's services to and from Beith RNAD to Kilmarnock, Dalry, Barrmill, Gateside and Lochwinnoch were taken over by Garnock Valley Coaches, Kilbirnie. However, no further vehicles passed to the operator.

Northern applied in August 1954 to reduce their Glasgow-Birmingham and Edinburgh-London services to operate seasonally only from immediately prior to Easter 1955 until the end of September, requesting withdrawal from 30th September 1954. BMMO, Ribble and North Western Road Car had been successful in obtaining a licence for a daily direct overnight service from Coventry to Glasgow, which included a pick up and set down in Birmingham, in November

Extract from –
"THE STAR"
May 27, 1953

PUBLIC ACKNOWLEDGEMENT

★

SCOTTISH-LONDON ROAD SERVICES

★

The Directors of NORTHERN ROADWAYS LIMITED desire to acknowledge the many expressions of goodwill received on their success in their efforts to establish their overnight Pullman express services between Glasgow—Edinburgh and London, now approved by the recent decision of H.M. Minister of Transport, and to express their sincere thanks to their many friends who supported them so wholeheartedly in their cause for improved long distance coach services.

NORTHERN ROADWAYS LIMITED will continue to improve the standard of their services in comfort and efficiency to justify the confidence expressed in them by the many thousands of passengers who have already used the services

The Scottish-London services continue to operate every night

Details of the services and reservations may be had from any approved Travel Agent or Kings Cross Coach Station, Judd-street, London, W.C.1 Terminus 7373, or TRAVEL TRIPE LIMITED, Tourist and Travel Agents, 22 Renfield-street, Glasgow, C.2, Telephone No City 7871, 50 Hanover-street, Edinburgh, Telephone No Caledonian 3511, and 77/79 Cadzow-street Hamilton, Telephone No 641.

HARRY McGHEE,
Managing Director

Northern Roadways,
20 Renfield Street,
GLASGOW, May, 1953.

1953, after the original earlier application had been refused. This was actually an extension of the existing Manchester service in which Western SMT had a share and which will be mentioned in more detail later. One of the advantages of the Northern service was the direct link to Birmingham which was only previously available with changes of vehicles on services from Glasgow. With the granting of this licence some eighteen months after the original application, despite Northern's objections, some of that advantage was removed. However, the competitors did not offer hostess service or a coach with reclining seats and toilet.

The Scottish Bus Group and the Railway Executive considered whether to object or not, as there was risk that by pushing Northern to continue with the services, they would gain a greater foothold in the market available but, in the event, they lodged an objection. One view was that Northern was merely trying to extract the 'cream' of the traffic, having originally fought to operate a year round service. In the event, Northern decided to withdraw their application on 16th October 1954. Harry McGhee admitted at the time that the company 'have had a sticky time on capital'. However, as a result of a number of talks with their agents and after further considering the pros and cons he reported that they had reconsidered their decision and would continue to run their services during the winter months.

Contract services –
a return to its roots

Until the early 'fifties, the contract services were largely maintained by Bedford OWBs, supplemented by vehicles from the coach fleet and the five double-deckers mentioned earlier. However, in 1954, a large quantity of second-hand double-deckers were acquired from a number of sources. Four former Glasgow vehicles, two wartime Albions and two pre-war AEC Regents were acquired, the first two via Millburn Motors, and the other two via Lowland Motorways, another Glasgow independent (in which Millburn, incidentally, had a financial interest).

It is, of course, important to remember that Millburn Motors, the biggest Scottish dealer in second-hand buses and coaches, could not be tapped as a source for many of the vehicles available, because they handled much of the

Scottish Bus Group stock, especially for Western SMT and Alexanders. Although some ex-Scottish Bus Group stock had been acquired in the early days, including Bedford OWBs which had been registered for Alexanders, but never used, since Northern's perceived predatory expansion of the 1940s and early 1950s, the Scottish Bus Group had operated strict rules with dealers, requiring them to provide undertakings that vehicles would not be sold to competitors. Of course, this did not stop Millburn selling other non-Scottish Bus Group stock to companies like Northern, thus allowing the ex-Glasgow Corporation Albions to be acquired.

No such restrictions applied to the major purchase of 40 second-hand Daimlers (COG5s) and Leylands (seven TD6cs and two TD7cs), obtained from Birmingham Corporation via Birds, the Stratford-on-Avon based dealer. A number of similar vehicles were also acquired via A&C McLennan of Spittalfield. These acquisitions signalled two changes. Firstly, Northern's move to a largely double-deck contract operation and, secondly, the introduction of a new livery of two-tone green with these vehicles. Initially, these vehicles operated in three liveries. Some were pressed into service in Birmingham colours, some retained McLennan's livery and some were painted in the new two tone green livery, with a few carrying 'Glengarrys' and a small number of the batch receiving the Northern scroll fleet name along their sides, though most operated anonymously, save for the legal lettering.

There had also been plans to purchase some double-deckers from Northern General Transport and five drivers were sent down to collect them. However, they were refused permission to collect them as no contract had been signed. A hurried phone call to W Eagleson (Chief Engineer for Northern at the time) was made and he requested the drivers to wait for him. He arrived from Glasgow in his Rover 90, packed the five drivers into his car and drove them to Birmingham where five double-deckers were collected from the Corporation, being part of the batch handled through Birds. Jimmy Connor was one of these drivers and he recalled suffering the misfortune of a breakdown shortly after starting the journey north, caused by leaking water hose connections. It was agreed that the rest of the convoy would head north; Jimmy stayed overnight, effected the repairs and drove home the next day. He was met

EOG 200, another of the ex-Birmingham Daimler COG5s is seen fully painted in Northern two tone green livery, complete with Northern scroll fleet name, running along the north side of George Square, Glasgow. In most cases, the destination box was not used and was normally painted over or carried a permanently painted 'Private'. Many of the batch had quite long lives, some surviving with Northern until the late 1950s. The batch of Daimlers were the closest Northern Roadways ever came to a standardised fleet and, even when they were in operation, there were always other vehicle types operating alongside them.

Ex-Birmingham Corporation Daimler COG5 FOF 234, still in its previous owner's livery with the coat of arms simply painted out, is parked at Buchanan Street Railway Station, loaded with what appears to be army personnel, in company with another former Birmingham vehicle which had received the new two tone green livery. Bringing up the rear is one of the Bedford OWBs (EGG 791) bought new by Northern and wearing the silver grey livery, fleet name and 'Glengarrys'. It is likely that the OWB had spent a period of its time on the RNAD contract at Beith. The carriage of military personnel continued to be undertaken by Northern, albeit on a relatively small scale.

With the obtaining of the contract for transporting school children from the new Glasgow housing schemes to the existing schools, Northern had to source vehicles from more than one location. BDR 274 was one of five Leyland TD5cs with Weymann bodies built in 1938/9 obtained from AMCC (Dealer) London, having originated with Plymouth Corporation, the others being ADR 808, BDR 256,261, 270 and 272. The bus, in silver grey rather than the new two tone green livery, has Knightswood set in its destination box, although it is travelling eastwards in the opposite direction, along the north side of George Square. Three Leyland TD4cs, also ex-Plymouth, were obtained at the same time from AMCC (JY 5003, 5007 and 9428) . A Glasgow Corporation AEC Regent III with Weymann bodywork (A166) is running in the opposite direction. (Geoff Morant)

with howls of protest from more senior drivers who were not given the chance of an overnight stay. Jimmy's response was that he was younger, fitter and more able to fix the fault than some of his older colleagues.

Further second-hand double-deckers were sourced during 1954 from Plymouth Corporation (three TD4cs and six TD5cs) via AMCC, the London dealer, plus three double-deckers from Ferguson of Renfrew. The vehicles were purchased from Ferguson when their operations (which included a share in the Paisley to Renfrew Ferry service) were acquired by Cunningham's Bus Service, Paisley. Interestingly, the Plymouth vehicles were painted in the silver grey livery, rather than the new green paint scheme.

Although the express services were the glamorous and most publicised aspect of their operations in the early 'fifties, much of their 'bread and butter' income now came from the growing demand for the transportation of school children, for which these double-deckers had been purchased. Post war, Glasgow had embarked on an ambitious scheme to re-house much of the central population of the city from their slums in areas like Gorbals to huge new housing estates such as Castlemilk and Easterhouse on the outskirts. New schools were not provided in the estates in those early days and, thus, school children had to be transported over considerable distances to the existing establishments. Northern obtained the important school contract from Glasgow Corporation and services were provided between areas such as Drumchapel and Partick, Castlemilk and Gorbals, Easterhouse and Bridgeton, Garthamlock and Dalmarnock. Buses were sometimes parked up at the schools during the day in preparation for either further transport during the day to locations such as swimming baths etc or ready for homewards travel at night. For example, Notre Dame RC School in Prince Albert Road could have up to 15 vehicles lined up to transport school children at home time. As an indication of the volume of traffic, around 40 buses (mostly double-deckers) were observed on Aitkenhead Road one afternoon carrying children.

Express Services – the struggle to keep going

Northern made increasing use of hired-in coaches to maintain their long distance express services as more of their own fleet was sold. The remains of their own express coach fleet began to look increasingly tired. Napier is believed to have pushed to recover the considerable finance he had put into the company. By the end of 1954, the directors were given as Harry McGhee and A O McGhee, indicating that Napier no longer had an interest.

By the end of 1954, most of the front-line express coach fleet and much of the private hire fleet had been sold, a process which had accelerated since 1953, although the pride of the fleet, the Daimler Freeline, remained amongst others. Late in the year, four of the remaining Burlingham Seagull-bodied AEC Regal IVs were sold to Bluebird of Hull. Almost immediately, these were hired back in Bluebird's livery, still with their original facilities, and continued to operate the long distance express services. A similar exercise appears to have happened with two of the Burlingham Seagull Leyland Royal Tigers which were sold to the operator, Cowell of Sunderland in 1954 and again hired back, in 1955. Garelochhead Coach Services are also known to have, occasionally, hired back one of the AEC Regal IV coaches purchased from Northern. Generally, the arrangement was to keep these vehicles with the same 32-seat layout plus toilet in which they had operated with Northern. Sometimes, the coaches would be driven by their own staff, but the second driver was often provided by Northern. It is also believed that coaches sold to Millburn were hired back prior to their sale to these operators.

On occasions, coaches were hired from other English operators. J.T. Whittle and Son, who were based at Kidderminster at the time, provided a coach for a journey from Birmingham to Glasgow and return in early August 1955 , probably due to the breakdown of a Northern vehicle.. They also provided coaches for a number of journeys from Glasgow to London during that month (at around £30 per journey coach hire rate excluding fuel).

A number of other smaller operators provided vehicles on a regular basis, including Weirs of Old Kilpatrick, McDowall of Kirkintilloch, Harkins of Glasgow and Yuille of Larkhall. Yuille bought a number of the ex-Northern Burlingham coaches from Bluebird of Hull and Cowell of Sunderland and hired these back to Northern from 1955 until the sale of the express service operations.

The practice of coach hiring was an integral part of the associated Travel Trips business and,

AEC Regal IV coach JGE 425 is seen running on hire to Northern, having been sold to Garelochead Coach Services (and named Loch Maree) in 1953, retaining its reclining seats and toilet, along with two of the same batch still running with Northern (JGD 110 and JGE 422) . JGD 110 would pass a year later, along with JGD 112, JGD 116 and JGE 419, to Bluebird of Hull and then be hired back in similar fashion, whilst JGE 422 passed to Dodds of Troon late in 1953. *(Ian Maclean Collection)*

AEC Regal IV JGE 422, as mentioned, was sold to Dodds of Troon via Millburn Motors in October 1953 and was up-seated to a 37-seater, with the removal of the toilet etc. It did not return on hire to Northern Roadways, unlike many of the original batch of express coaches.

in practice, did not present any major difficulties. Logistical problems with the type of coaches hired were more likely to present the challenges. Where vehicles hired did not have toilets, storage or a hot water boiler, toilet stops were made for passengers at suitable locations. Harkins, for example, supplied a Perkins diesel-engined Bedford on occasion. The hostess would store the food boxes, blankets etc on the back seat and hand these out at the start of the journey but, of course, only cold drinks could be supplied.

Nevertheless, there were still examples of the company attempting to expand in other directions. In early 1955, in an interesting twist, Northern identified an opportunity to make further use for their large fleet of double-deckers, when Glasgow Corporation was suffering a shortage of both vehicles and drivers. Northern this time approached Glasgow and offered both buses and drivers and Glasgow Corporation set up a sub-committee to consider the suggestion. Sadly, nothing came of this approach, no doubt due in part, at least, to municipal pride.

The Helen Street, Govan premises were vacated early in 1955 and the fleet and staff moved to an old Foundry in Crown Point Road in the east end of Glasgow. It was said that if you dropped a coin onto the ground, you had no chance of finding it; such was the level of dust and dirt remaining from its previous use, hardly helpful to keeping the fleet in good order. A fuel pump was set up and vehicles were washed outside in the yard.

A degree of relief was provided in 1955 when the London based company of Tartan Arrow, which provided removals and cargo haulage services north of the border, purchased a new coach. This AEC Reliance with bulbous Bellhouse Hartwell coachwork was fitted out with 30 reclining seats and a toilet and hired out to Northern Roadways on a permanent basis in a livery of white and light brown, driven by a Tartan Arrow employed driver. Normally, the coach was only driven by this employee, making it a very long shift for him; no tachographs in those days. This coach suffered a major accident after a relatively short period of operation and was converted for use by Tartan Arrow as a removals van.

During the period 1955-6, terminal points were changed in both Birmingham and Glasgow. In September 1955 the Birmingham terminal point was changed from Smithfield Garage to Allenways Coach Station in Park Street, which was also near to the Bull Ring. In Glasgow, Lowland Motorways, another go-ahead Glasgow independent in which the Sandersons, who owned Millburn Motors, had a financial interest, opened an impressive travel centre at 192 Buchanan Street, Glasgow. Booking for all major express services was made available, including the Scottish Bus Group, various English operators such as Associated Motorways and Northern Roadways. In April 1956 Northern applied to change their terminal points for their Glasgow to Bournemouth, Glasgow to Birmingham and Glasgow to London Kings Cross Coach Station services respectively in Glasgow to the travel centre at 192 Buchanan Street. The new terminus was close to the Scottish Bus Group's Buchanan Street Bus Station, giving Northern a far more central and suitable site. At the same time, return fares were to be increased from £4 12s 6d to £5 for Bournemouth, single £1 12 6d to £1 16s 0d and return from £2 17s 6d to £3 15s 0d on the Birmingham service on Friday, Saturday and Sunday night services for the period from Friday preceding Whit Monday until 30th September with a return fare of £3-15-0 to £4 for the London service. No objections were raised by Western and the changes were granted in May 1956, although Northern do not appear to have used the new Glasgow terminal point.

In February 1956 Scottish Airlines took over the Glasgow St Enoch to Prestwick Airport service, operated by Northern Roadways in connection with Isle of Man flights. The application was granted in March 1956, subject to the fares being increased to meet Western's objection.

Further retraction occurred in March 1956 with the cancellation of the excursions and tours licence starting from Clydebank. David Lawson already had an extensive excursions and tours licence from the town and surrounding areas.

Another move of the fleet was made in early 1956 from Crown Point Road to the old gas works yard at 122 Dalmarnock Road, as some partial demolition of some of the foundry buildings was being undertaken. An open yard provided the base for the contract fleet together, allowing the abandonment of the Hyndland premises. The yard had a couple of sheds for maintenance work and various outbuildings, to which a raised inspection pit and fuel pump was added.

Hiring back coaches still equipped for express service duty became normal practice in 1955/6 and their movement between companies became quite complex. AEC Regal IV JGE 421 and Leyland Royal Tiger JGE 427 were two coaches which were sold to Cowell of Sunderland in 1954, along with Regal IV JGE 420 and the other three Leyland Royal Tigers (JGE 428-30) . JGE 420 and 428 were hired back to Northern by Cowell but these two are not recorded as being hired. Nevertheless, they did come back 'north of the border' to Yuille of Larkhall, with whom Northern Roadways worked closely, and were hired back again for use on the express services in 1955/6 in a two tone green livery, along with JGE 419 (purchased from Bluebird of Hull) , JGE 420 and 428, crewed by Northern Roadways as usual, retaining their toilet, boiler etc. (Garry Ward Collection)

Tartan Arrow were a well known freight carrier, operating between England and Scotland in the 1950s. In 1955, they moved into passenger transport with the purchase of a new AEC Reliance coach with Bellhouse Hartwell 30-seater coachwork, plus toilet. This poor photograph is the only known view of PYU 4 which was hired out exclusively to Northern Roadways for their express services. It had a short life, being badly damaged in an accident and was converted to a removals van for further use by Tartan Arrow.

Express Services –
the final days and sell out

The Edinburgh to London service had always suffered from the dead mileage and cost incurred in operating the positioning journeys. In the winter time, when loadings were lower, a coach would be sent with one driver to Edinburgh, where he would pick up the passengers and proceed to Penrith. During the stopover period at Penrith, passengers and luggage would be transferred onto the Glasgow-London coaches. The Northern driver would then make himself comfortable with blankets (and, hopefully, get some sleep) whilst awaiting the arrival of the north bound convoy of coaches. When they arrived, Edinburgh passengers and luggage would be transferred onto his coach and taken northwards, thus saving one coach making the long haul to London lightly loaded. At other times, when loadings were limited to a couple of people, Northern Roadways would arrange for Allan of Gorebridge to send a car or small bus from Edinburgh and transport the passengers to Abington or, occasionally, Penrith, where they would be transferred on to a London bound coach. On 6th April 1956, Northern ceased to operate the Edinburgh to London route and arrangements were made for pre-booked passengers to be carried by the rival SOL service. The licence was subsequently cancelled.

Towards the end of express service operation, drivers were warned not to allow any strangers onto their coaches in case they were Sheriff's Officers intent on impounding the coach. This may relate to a court case raised by Birds of Stratford-upon-Avon with regard to outstanding payment for six ex-Birmingham Daimlers purchased between September and November 1954, plus some subsequent spare Daimler radiators, amounting to over £2,200. Western SMT's Minutes of 30th July 1956 recorded that in recent months Northern had only been able to maintain their long distance express services by hiring-in from small independent operators. A number of these operators were forming themselves into a syndicate and had made a firm offer of £25,000 for the services. Although it has never been confirmed which operators these were, its likely to have been those who regularly hired vehicles

to the company, including Yuille of Larkhall and McDowall, Harkins and, possibly, Grant Brothers, all of Glasgow. When the Northern Edinburgh to London service ceased, Mr McGhee promised that, in the event of him disposing of his remaining express services he would give Scottish Omnibuses Ltd first refusal, which he had now done. Immediate payments from the independent operators was due within five days and after long discussions acquisition was recommended at that sum. According to the minutes, members of the Scottish Bus Group were precluded from taking shares in Northern, but they could acquire the goodwill and assets. Permission was requested from the Commission and was approved on the following Thursday (9th August 1956).

However, this was not the first instance of Northern Roadways offering to sell out. Through intermediaries, Harry McGhee had approached the Scottish Bus Group in October 1953, offering to sell out completely. At that time it was known that the company was experiencing financial difficulties in carrying on the business. Revenue on the London services was estimated to be not less than £96,000 per annum, whilst the Birmingham service was estimated at £16,000 per annum. Revenue for the latter service was expected to double in the next year with the granting in the licence to carry two-way traffic. Private hire business was acknowledged to be very important, some £40,000 being earned per year. By then, the company was stated to own 'no vehicles', having to sell them to pay off bank overdrafts and relying totally on hiring vehicles. Whilst the express fleet had been reduced by then (and would reduce further in the next two years) and much of the private hire fleet had been sold off, the statement that no vehicles were owned at that time, whatever its origin was not correct.

Based on an anticipated annual revenue of £168,000, McGhee offered to sell the operations for £55,000. The offer was based on the sale of the Travel Trips premises in Hanover Street, Edinburgh for £20,000 (and renting them back to Travel Trips at £1,000 rent per annum), a 'special commission' of £5,000 per annum for five years, in addition to appointment of Travel Trips as travel agents for the Scottish Bus Group and the provision of standard agency fees, plus a further £10,000. Interestingly, the Helen Street depot was not offered as part of the sale. The Scottish

Bus Group, after a long discussion, decided to approach the British Transport Commission and asked them for a decision on whether to proceed.

The BTC decided, on that occasion, not to pursue the matter and Northern Roadways were informed some three weeks later. It is probable that the Commission and the Scottish Bus Group did not expect Northern Roadways to survive much longer. The fact that the express services were kept going in difficult circumstances for nearly three more years to survive and have their goodwill sold is a tribute to the staff and management.

The real threat of the express services being acquired by a consortium of independents must have concentrated the minds and this time, the Scottish Bus Group and British Transport Commission acted promptly to acquire the operations. The other key difference was that only the express services and some excursions and tours licences were to be acquired. Northern Roadways' large contract operations, their Strathpeffer tours from Glasgow and their private hire work were not included as part of the deal.

Working on the Express Services

Some aspects of the express operations have already been mentioned above. However, some further detail is worthy of inclusion. Shifts on the express services were long, staff signing on an hour before coach departure time at the depot, to stock up the vehicle, fuel the coach if necessary, fill the boiler through a roof-mounted plug and check the coach over. If the crew were allocated to the Edinburgh service, they would sign on some two hours before scheduled departure from the capital city, to give them sufficient time to operate 'light' from Glasgow. Drivers normally worked three return trips every two weeks.

The recollections from former employees of the company give a picture of what it was like to be involved in the express services. Miss Findlay worked in the accounts department of Northern Roadways in the early 'fifties. On one occasion, she was asked to help out as a stewardess on the Glasgow-London 'Pullman' coach service and, after about three minutes tuition was left to 'get on with it'. She was sent to the Helen Street, Govan depot to collect her uniform. The principal

qualification was to be tall enough to carry the huge teapot down the aisle of the bus without catching the heads of passengers or cover them in hot tea. The food was prepared and packaged by a high quality baker, Strachans of Pollokshields. One of the duties of the stewardess was to ensure that the boiler was switched on before they left Glasgow in order that there was enough water to make tea by Lockerbie. The drivers could obtain food for themselves at stops where catering facilities were available, but where this was not feasible could avail themselves of the food cartons supplied to passengers. Drivers and stewardesses travelled overnight one night and returned the next, retiring to accommodation in London on completion of their journey to get some sleep before the return journey home. In the early days a public house on Pentonville Road was regularly used; in later days accommodation in Argyll Square was substituted.

The Birmingham express service was viewed as an 'easier duty'. Overnight accommodation was not provided on this service, staff often going to the cinema to occupy themselves for a few hours during the day after completing their duties, prior to returning north that night. Miss Findlay was a stewardess on three occasions on the London service and also once on the Birmingham run. She recalled that Northern had a post of chief stewardess. When this lady left the company the post was re-advertised for someone who had three languages, very much in the vogue of air stewardesses on which the service was modelled, but a bit of an 'overkill', given that the vast majority of their passengers were British.

As each new coach arrived, the staff speculated if they would get paid, as mentioned earlier, but they did and there were 'perks' to the job, staff being given reduced rate travel on Travel Trips tours which were lightly loaded. Reduced cost travel was also given on air travel to places like the Isle of Man from Prestwick through the Travel Trips agency. The principal 'flagship' coach tour which the agency advertised from Glasgow was based on the Ben Wyvis hotel. An assortment of Northern Roadways coaches were used on the tours, including their Bedford OBs and Plaxton-bodied Maudslays. Although staff could sometimes travel on this tour at reduced rates if bookings were light, they were also asked to help staff the hotel from time to time, Miss Findlay once

A stewardess runs through her check list in the Helen Street store room where tartan rugs, pillow cases, biscuit tins and large tea urns are evident. She was responsible for ensuring that her coach was stocked up prior to departure, whilst the drivers checked over the vehicle and ensured it was fuelled etc. *(Robert Grieves Collection)*

The smart uniforms worn by the Stewardesses is evident from this view inside one of the Burlingham bodied coaches. She is loading the food boxes in an overhead shelf around the storage cupboard area. This would be her working area during the journey, whilst breaks would be taken on the back seat to the right of the toilet. *(Robert Grieves Collection)*

A passenger's eye view looking back into one of the coaches. Some sleep on as the coach refuels with 'derv' at Moore's Garage near Doncaster on a London bound journey, whilst the hostess would be providing a hot drink to those awake. *(John C Gillham Collection)*

Northern made much of the practicality of carrying young children unattended on their express services with availability of a stewardess on board. One young child is lifted off a coach at the Glasgow terminus at the end of a journey from London. *(Garry Ward Collection)*

working as a receptionist there. It was renowned for its excellent food.

Many of the coach drivers were drawn from ex-forces personnel. Much tours traffic emanated from Travel Trips and other companies were sub-contracted to provide coaches, including Cotters of Glasgow (with whom they were in competition at times), especially at the popular holiday times like the September weekend, when many vehicles travelled to Blackpool.

In the early days, breakdowns were very rare (drivers being instructed to phone the home depot if there was a problem) but, as more of the front line fleet was sold and efforts were made to keep costs to a minimum, the remainder of the fleet was being used ever more intensively and fault repair was not always undertaken quickly. From around 1954, increasing problems were experienced, with mechanics leaving and not being replaced. On one trip the drivers were provided with a 40 gallon water tank to keep the radiator system topped up, as a cracked engine block had not been attended to; on that occasion, the mechanic told one of the drivers not to tell his mate. The coach heating systems sometimes froze up because of the lack of anti-freeze in the system. Drivers were known to put pillows over their head to keep themselves warm; it must have been some sight. One of the methods to keep warm on a lightly loaded coach was to hang blankets across the back half of the coach to reduce draughts. Not, perhaps, the image of a prestigious express coach operation.

On occasions, the drivers needed all their ingenuity to keep their vehicles going as the following couple of stories will illustrate. Whilst heading north over Shap with the Daimler Freeline, the driver heard moans from passengers. He switched the internal lights on whilst still driving but could not detect any problems. However, he pulled in at a closed petrol station on Strawberry Bank (the first major climb northwards) and, having left his seat to investigate further, discovered that the coach was filling with smoke. Passengers and stewardess were evacuated whilst the problem was investigated further. On lifting of the engine inspection covers, he determined that water had been leaking into a cylinder from a crack in the cylinder wall. When he tried to start the engine again, there was no success. With a bunch of stranded passengers, not to mention crew, on one of the bleakest parts of the Pennines, drastic action

was called for. With the electrics switched on he rolled the coach back down the A6 for a hundred yards or so and managed to start it by engaging reverse gear, effectively kick starting it.

Another tale from those days, illustrating the spirit of keeping the service going, concerned a Birmingham run when the driver noticed around Preston that the fuel gauge was showing a very low reading. Having confirmed that it was working, he pulled into a closed petrol station. By good fortune, a friend was driving a lorry in the opposite direction and stopped to establish what the problem was. The two friends 'borrowed' a length of hose from the garage and siphoned off 20 gallons of diesel to allow them to complete their journey. On another Birmingham journey the coach broke down at Warrington. Jimmy Connor and Bill McDonald were the drivers and Jimmy struggled to repair the vehicle but realised that further work would be needed. They contacted a local operator and arranged for them to provide a coach and driver to Birmingham, with a return that evening to Warrington, whilst they organised repairs. Having undertaken the repair they phoned Glasgow and advised the actions taken. On checking the operator used, the drivers were praised for their actions, particularly as this operator had not been used before and was likely to be facing a long wait for payment of the bill!

Journeys over the Pennines were hazardous in winter time, both Shap on the A6 and Bowes Moor on the A66 being prone to heavy snowfalls and icy conditions. Trucks would often slip and slide on the many difficult sections of the route, as would Northern's coaches and they would help to dig each other out of drifts. It was said that truck drivers would always help a Northern Roadways vehicle because they knew they could get a hot drink and a sandwich from the crew.

The constraints of the express service licences gave them no room for expansion and, it would appear, insufficient revenue to replace the fleet. Staff who had originally been provided with uniforms often latterly had to wear their own clothing or buy a uniform for themselves. Stewardesses obtained a change of uniform once a year but drivers were not so lucky. When London Transport were disposing of old uniforms Northern Roadways purchased a quantity and express service drivers were summoned to the office to pick from two canvas bags. They made the best of the sizes of clothes obtained, sometimes with pretty amusing results.

Inevitably, there were occasional accidents. AEC Regal IV JGD 113 had a particularly bad smash and was brought back to Glasgow then returned to Burlingham's in Blackpool for major coachwork repair. Arriving back in Glasgow, it was taken out for a run by a second mechanic, only to have its rear offside run into by another vehicle, resulting in further repair work being needed. When completed, it returned to service and was one of only a couple of original coaches that remained to maintain the services until sale of the express licences.

Another accident reported by a local paper in August 1955, referred to a coach on the Bournemouth service which was passing through Hursley Road in Chandlers Ford, near Southampton, when the driver was hailed by a passing cyclist after he had seen smoke coming from the rear of the vehicle. The full coach load plus drivers and hostess quickly clambered clear and, within minutes, the vehicle was reported to be ablaze. Eastleigh-based firemen quickly arrived and got the fire under control and passengers luggage was salvaged from the boot. The cause of the fire was reported to have been 'over-heated oil in the brake drums'.

Only one fatality is known to have occurred in five years of operation when another of the AEC Regal IV coaches crashed one frosty night into a hump backed bridge near Newark and the driver was killed. Thankfully, the coach was lightly-loaded. The second driver and hostess were asleep on the front nearside seat rather than the usual rear location and were thrown clear of the coach which split open at the first nearside window bay.

Passengers' luggage is unloaded from JGE 421 at the Blytheswood Square terminus in Glasgow. The coach is showing signs of the 400 mile winter journey north and the shovel propped against the rear would have been put to good use during severe winter weather when snow and ice could quickly accumulate, especially on the journey over the A66 around Bowes Moor. Lorry drivers quickly learned that they would be rewarded with a hot cup of tea if they helped to keep a Northern Roadways coach moving in the tricky conditions. It is likely that Tartan Arrow would have learned about Northern's services during these days, possibly encouraging them to provide their own coach on the services. *(Garry Ward Collection)*

Express Services takeover and the Birmingham problem

Formal agreement to take over the services was reported in August 1956 and a £7,500 deposit was paid, pending the transfer of the licences. None of the few remaining vehicles involved in express and tour operations was involved in the takeover. The last southbound Birmingham service, using one of Northern's few remaining coaches, had three passengers on it, including Frank Palmer from Western SMT, who took note of the driver changeover points.

A month later, it was reported that agreement had been reached with Travel Trips, appointing the latter as booking agents for the company for a period of five years from 1st September 1956. By the time of the takeover of Northern's licences in 1956, Travel Trips would appear to have only had their premises at 22 Renfield Street, Glasgow. Bookings for the Edinburgh service, for example, were referred to Sanderson's Travel Service, 22 Coates Crescent, Edinburgh. They remained as booking agents for the Scottish Bus Group until 1972.

The takeover included some of the excursion and tours licences, in addition to the express services and the first moves related to these were made in August 1956 when Scottish Omnibuses Ltd applied for the excursions and tours licence from Queen Street, Edinburgh to Strathpeffer (2, 7 and 14 day tours), Bridlington (7 days) and Ramsgate (9 days) and a switch of terminus to The Mound, which was granted in September 1956. Two months later, they applied to change the Edinburgh terminus of the tours again, this time to St Andrews Square from the Mound.

As Western SMT were existing operators on the Glasgow to London service, the Northern licence was simply cancelled in October 1956. To cover for the additional traffic, Western applied in September 1956 to increase duplication on the London service by six vehicles in any one day from October to April and Tuesday to Thursday May to September (and eight on other days plus mid December to mid-January and Glasgow Spring holidays) and the primary application was granted on 27th October 1956. With the cessation of Northern's London Service, the hostess service

providing light food and drinks also disappeared and it was to be nearly 25 years before it returned in the early days of express service deregulation of the 1980s. Cotters, another long-standing Glasgow independent, re-introduced food and hot drinks on a new express service, together with on-board videos, followed by the Scottish Bus Group and their equivalent 'Cordon Bleu' service.

Scottish Omnibuses Ltd (who traded under the SMT fleet name) made further licence applications to take over Northern Roadways' Glasgow to Birmingham and Bournemouth services and to switch the Glasgow terminus to Buchanan Street Bus Station. Application was also made to take over Northern Roadways' Glasgow-based excursions and tours licences to Bridlington (7 days), Ramsgate (9 days), Colintraive day tour and Prestwick Airport day tour. All applications were granted in October 1956.

Together with the Glasgow to London licence, Northern Roadways cancelled their Glasgow to Birmingham and Bournemouth licences in October 1956. However, the Birmingham cancellation was rescinded a month later. BMMO, North Western Road Car, Ribble Motor Services (and the Birmingham police) objected to the takeover by Scottish Omnibuses Ltd (SOL) of the Northern Roadways Glasgow to Birmingham licence. At the same time, BMMO, North Western Road Car and Ribble applied for a new express service from Birmingham (Digbeth) to Glasgow (Port Dundas) to replace the Northern Roadways service. SOL, Western SMT, British Railways and, again, Birmingham Police provided counter objections.

Thus, to protect their newly acquired interests, SOL continued to operate under the Northern Roadways licence, albeit from Buchanan Street, Glasgow to Birmingham. The SOL service was advertised as being operated 'in conjunction with Northern Roadways'. Alexander-bodied AEC Regal IV coaches with toilets, primarily used on London services, were operated from the SOL garage in Airdrie and the hostess service provided by Northern maintained to comply with the Northern licence conditions, providing an advertised service of 'reclining seats, tea and light snacks throughout the journey' though no coaches were retro-fitted with boilers; in practice, cold drinks were served. Three 'London' AEC Regal IVs were allocated to Airdrie by March 1957 (B439/40 HWS 941/2 of 1951 and newly

Scottish Omnibuses Limited used AEC Regal IV coaches similar to HWS 946, fitted with toilets and 30 reclining seats, on the Birmingham and Bournemouth express services taken over from Northern Roadways. These restrained though attractive Alexander-bodied vehicles make an interesting comparison with the Burlingham Seagull-bodied coaches used by Northern. This particular coach was on the SMT London to Edinburgh 2 day West Coast service and is parked at Oxford. *(Garry Ward Collection)*

rebodied B456 KSC 53, built in 1953). SOL also had an AEC Reliance with Alexander 30-seat coach body, fitted with a toilet (NSF 543) and this is likely to have been used on occasion, as it spent a period allocated to Airdrie Garage.

The Birmingham applications had considerable history and complexity. Negotiations were concluded with Ribble Motor Services in February 1952 to acquire an interest in the Glasgow to Manchester night service which was solely licensed to and operated by Ribble Motor Services (their Blackpool, Manchester and Liverpool day services were all jointly operated with Western SMT). However, circumstances prevented this agreement being put into effect and, when Ribble applied for a night service from Coventry to Glasgow, primarily to counter Northern Roadways Birmingham service, due to restrictions on the primary licence granted, they intended to continue the night service licence under their control. The service application was, effectively, for an extension of the existing Manchester service. Western had not originally

opposed this application but the granting of a Coventry to Glasgow service would have provided Ribble with two services solely licensed to them. Western decided instead to pursue the purchase of Ribble's operational interests north of Carlisle for £15,000, which had been the original approach proposed in 1951, when Ribble's interests were first reviewed. The Coventry to Glasgow service was ultimately granted in November 1953, despite objections from Northern Roadways. Normally, operation of the service was shared between Ribble and Midland Red, with North Western Road Car and Western SMT providing duplicates, all operators using standard non-toilet coaches.

Ribble finally responded in October 1954, offering to surrender their interests north of the border for an increased price of £29,500. However, the Scottish Bus Group Directors decided to leave the matter in abeyance at that time.

Western reported in their minutes of 29th October 1956 that SOLs application to take over Northern's Glasgow to Birmingham service had attracted objections from Ribble, BMMO and

North Western Road Car and the same operators had made their own applications for a Birmingham to Glasgow service which Western objected to. The Scottish Bus Group Chairman proposed merging Northern's service with the existing Ribble Glasgow to Coventry service, with the effect of relinquishing of Ribble's interest north of the border (from the night Glasgow-Manchester-Birmingham-Coventry services).

The Scottish Bus Group noted that there had been considerable development of night traffic between Glasgow and Birmingham. Effectively, the Scottish Bus Group proposed to purchase the Scottish part of the Glasgow to Manchester service and sell to Ribble the English parts of the ex-Northern Roadways Glasgow to Birmingham service. Western's minutes of 27th December 1956 reported that the above arrangements had been agreed at a price of around £22,000, which finally removed the anomaly of purely Ribble licensed services operating north of the border.

Scottish Omnibuses continued to operate what they termed the 'Sleeper night coach service' until September 1957 operating under the licence acquired from Northern, leaving at 8pm in either direction and arriving at 8:00pm the following day. The Birmingham terminal point was eventually changed to Midland Red's Digbeth Coach Station from Allenways Coach Terminal. The original Northern licence was finally surrendered for the start of the winter period in October 1957 and, at that point, the hostess service and London type toilet coaches ceased to be used.

SOL then became an operating partner in the joint night service to Coventry, using standard coaches, and Birmingham travellers were denied the choice of a higher level service. Western SMT finally took over the SOL share of the licence in 1963, in anticipation of the delivery of new 36ft-long Leyland Leopards into their fleet.

The situation was different with the Bournemouth service. Scottish Omnibuses Ltd continued to offer the Glasgow to Bournemouth service as a 'Sleeper Night Coach'. It provided a valuable direct connection to Bournemouth, avoiding the need to make a number of coach changes via the Associated Motorways network at Cheltenham as mentioned earlier. The 1958 season Long Distance Services brochure quoted the service as operating on Fridays-only from 6th June until 19th September, leaving Buchanan Street at 6:00pm and arriving at Bournemouth (The Square Bus Station) 19 hours and 5 minutes later at 1:05pm (officially taking 30 minutes longer than the scheduled Northern service). The return journeys operated on Saturdays only from 14th June until 27th September, again leaving at 6:00pm and taking the same time. As there was no southbound journey on the last weekend, it is possible that one of the coaches used on the Edinburgh to London service, diverted to Bournemouth to provide the returning coach.

The original restrictions relating to carriage of passengers making a return journey from Glasgow to Bournemouth continued to apply. Toilet and washroom facilities were offered together with reclining seats and rugs, as available on the London service vehicles, and tea and light snacks were advertised as being provided without extra charge, the vehicles also being operated from SOL's Airdrie garage. By 1961, the service was leaving Glasgow at 5:45pm with a scheduled arrival in Bournemouth at 12:45pm the following day, reflecting, no doubt, the increased congestion on the ordinary roads that the service traversed. The return journey by then left at 10:00pm, with a scheduled arrival of 5:00pm the following day.

'Bread and Butter' operations

The last long-distance Northern coach to go was the pride of the fleet, the Duple Ambassador Daimler Freeline, sometime late in 1956, and so an era had ended.

The provision of school services for pupils in outlying Glasgow housing schemes continued to be the main operation, operated primarily by the large fleet of ex-Birmingham Daimler and Leyland double-deckers, together with the operation of some works services. Some of the fleet was also occupied during school time, providing transport to local swimming baths etc. At weekends, they provided buses for transporting football supporters, including those of the two big Glasgow teams, Celtic and Rangers, to matches. Members of the fleet could also regularly be seen during the Summer transporting children on Sunday School trips down the Clyde Coast to places such as Ayr and Prestwick. Transport of military personnel continued, maintaining a link with their original operations. Some additional revenue was also obtained with the placing of advertisements between decks, 'Flit with Pitt', a local removals firm, being a commonly used advert.

With the acquisition of the competitive element of Northern's operations, another source of work became available. SMT had frequent vehicle shortages at various depots, including Airdrie. They often hired-in buses from fellow Scottish Bus Group member Central SMT during the weekend at Airdrie, but also hired from Northern, who always had a proportion of vehicles available out with the school start and end times. Northern's vehicles could often be seen operating from Glasgow to Airdrie and points eastwards, from the mid-1950s onwards. Vehicles were crewed by SMT staff and carried the ubiquitous paper sticker destinations affixed to the front nearside windows, as Northern's vehicles generally had painted over screens carrying the legend 'Private' or, occasionally, empty screens. The green livery was an advantage as well, even if it wasn't the same shade as that of SMT.

Although Northern Roadways held the contract for provision of schools services, a number of small operators provided support on a sub-contract basis, including Grant Brothers of Glasgow and Auld of Elderslie. The vehicles used were normally painted in Northern's two tone green livery and, in the case of Auld, their buses were garaged in Northern's yard. On cessation of the express services, some of the express service drivers obtained employment with these companies. Through the years, vehicles regularly passed between Northern Roadways and the many small operators who assisted with coaches or provided school buses on sub-contract. There is speculation, as mentioned earlier, that at least some of these operators would have formed the consortium who were making an offer for Northern's express services.

Another advantage to the removal of the competitive element of Northern Roadways' operation, was the freedom to buy former Scottish Bus Group vehicles from Millburn Motors and Northern made full use of this opportunity. From

Auld of Elderslie was another operator who undertook sub-contracted school work for Northern Roadways. He parked his vehicles in Northern's Dalmarnock yard and, amongst the vehicles owned, were two ex-London Transport STL's DLU 250/1 (ex-STD 1894 and 1890) which had come from Yuille of Larkhall. Although former London Transport STs had operated on hire to Northern Roadways during the war, no STDs were ever owned by Northern. The vehicles had returned to Yuille by 1958 after the untimely death of the proprietor.

Auld operated his vehicles as non-PSVs and also purchased similar vehicles to Northern Roadways. GHA 999 was an ex-BMMO wartime Daimler CWA6 with Brush bodywork which had been rebuilt by Willowbrook in the early 1950s. A similar vehicle in Northern's fleet can be seen to the left. To the right, the rear of former Alexander Albion CX13 WG 9015 with Alexander body new in 1939 is captured. There is no record of this vehicle having operated, but it may have run for Auld prior to sale to Dodds of Lesmahagow in 1958.

The first batch of former Scottish Bus Group double-deckers acquired via Millburn Motors were six Daimlers and five Guy Arabs in 1956. ASD 120 was the only highbridge example amongst the Daimlers (in this case a CWG5 model new in 1943) It had been heavily rebuilt in 1950 by Western SMT, using stock Leyland parts, which greatly altered the appearance of its original Massey body. It was last licensed by Northern Roadways in September 1959.

The remaining five Daimlers acquired from Western SMT via Millburn (all CWA6s) had Brush or Duple lowbridge bodies and were new in 1943/4. ASD 713, a Duple-bodied example, photographed in a Glasgow suburb, would have cost around £250 from the Dealer and ran until 1958. Although there had been some rebuilding, including rubber mounting of upper-deck front windows, fitting of sliding vents in place of half drop windows and, it would appear, replacement of the wooden seats, it retained its basic utility profile. The Northern fleet name had been applied to both the side panel and also, unusually, to the panel above the destination box. In Western days, this panel would have carried the Western fleet name, illuminated at night by bulbs behind it.

Four of the Guys acquired in 1956 had lowbridge bodies by Massey or Weymann, but VS 4357 (which had started life in the Greenock Motor Services fleet) , new in 1945, had been rebodied by Western SMT with a second-hand Park Royal body from a former London Transport Guy which had been sent for rebodying. It is seen here on hire to SMT, devoid of fleet names, sitting outside the old Buchanan Street Bus Station.

1956 until their demise, they regularly purchased many ex-Scottish Bus Group vehicles, particularly Western SMT buses. First to arrive were a batch of wartime Daimlers and Guy Arabs in 1956 from Western. Thus, when SMT hired vehicles from Northern, they were often vehicles which had previously been owned by a fellow Scottish Bus Group member.

Towards the end of 1956, nine wartime Daimlers were purchased, four examples coming from BMMO, with their Duple or Weymann bodywork considerably rebuilt (by Willowbrook) and five coming from Rochdale Corporation, with more unusual ECW bodywork to their pre-war design.

Around this time, an unidentified Bristol K with post-war Weymann bodywork, from the Maidstone and District fleet, was also operated. Central SMT contributed two 20 year old Leyland TD4s as well, followed by further TD4s and some TD7s in 1957, all with Leyland bodies, and a couple of Leyland double-deckers also came from SMT. The general principle was to buy batches

of old double-deckers cheaply, which, ideally, had a couple of years CoF remaining on them. When their CoFs expired they were replaced by the next intake of vehicles and, generally, sold for scrap, although vehicles were transferred between some of the smaller operators with whom they closely worked, such as Yuille of Larkhall and Grant Brothers of Glasgow.

Sourced from further afield, six Northern Coachbuilders and Strachan rebodied Leyland TD4s were purchased from North (dealer) of Leeds in 1957, having originated with Devon General, although not all were used. The steady acquisition of these vehicles caused inroads to be made into the large batch of ex-Birmingham Daimlers and Leylands.

Tour operations from Glasgow to the Ben Wyvis Hotel continued, often using hired-in coaches. However, in 1957, a Duple-bodied Bedford SBO, JVD 623, which had been displayed at the 1953 Scottish Motor Show in Northern Roadways' colours but never delivered, was acquired from

Four Daimler COG6s with Eastern Coach Works H30/26R bodies were acquired from Rochdale Corporation early in 1957. EDK 689 was, numerically, the first, the others being EDK 690, 692 and 693. The curved trim strip running from the top deck to the driver's cab would have supported the streamlined blue and cream paint scheme used by Rochdale. This was over painted in the much simpler light green scheme used by Northern, together with the destination and route number boxes. It later passed to Bayliss of Creca near Annan for use in transporting workers for the building of Chapelcross Nuclear Power Station. It carries a 'Flit with Pitt' advert commonly carried on many Northern double-deckers for this removals company.

VS 3632 was a Leyland TD5 with Leyland H28/26R body new in 1937 obtained from Yuille, Larkhall, having originated with Greenock Motor Services and passing via Western SMT and Millburn Motors to Yuille. It was one of two Leylands to pass from Yuille to Northern Roadways in 1957 and is seen here in Myrtle Park, near Hampden Park on a football hire. *(Robert Grieves Collection)*

OKH 507 was one of two Bedford SBGs with Plaxton 35-seater bodies new in 1953 obtained from Bluebird of Hull in 1955, to whom Northern had sold and hired back some of their express coach fleet. The coach is at the Ben Wyvis Hotel, Strathpeffer on a tour in the mid 'fifties and returned to Bluebird, along with OKH 506 early in 1956. *(Robert Grieves Collection)*

The 1958 purchases included eight Guy Arabs which had originated with Western SMT, with a mixture of highbridge and lowbridge bodies. ASD 402 had Northern Counties L27/26R bodywork and was new in 1943. Like VS 4357 illustrated earlier, it was on hire to SMT from their Airdrie depot and the crew await their departure time at the stances outside Buchanan Street Bus Station. It was last licensed in October 1959.

Three ex-London Transport Guys were amongst the 1958 purchases from Western SMT, via Millburn Motors, all with Northern Counties H30/26R bodies and dating from 1945, having served less than five years with them. GYL 296 awaits a contingent of school children at an unknown location in the Glasgow area. The destination blind has the more usual 'PRIVATE' legend painted on.

Buses were parked up in the large depot yard at Dalmarnock gas works yard in between duties and it is inevitable that a considerable proportion of photographs were taken there. Three of the remaining four Guy Arabs acquired from Western via Millburn had started life with either Young's Bus Service or its subsidiary, Paisley and District. XS 5605 had originated with the latter in 1945 and, after withdrawal by Western SMT, went on loan to Central SMT before sale to Millburn, then Northern Roadways in April 1958. With a Certificate of Fitness expiring in October 1959, it served for around 18 months with Northern Roadways. It had a Roe L27/28R body of largely utility appearance, although the half drop windows had been replaced by sliding ones during its period with Western.

One of the oldest buses operated was a Leyland TD3 (CS 124) new in 1934 to Western SMT with Short Brothers bodywork which came to Northern Roadways in March 1959. The bus had been rebodied by Alexander in 1945 with a utility body having a strong resemblance to Leyland bodywork. Sister vehicle CS 125 was also acquired but its CoF had expired in that month and it was scrapped by Northern. CS 124 is running across Bridgeton Cross underneath a network of tram and trolleybus wires, with a Central SMT Northern Counties-bodied Leyland following behind. In the background can be seen street furniture from a bygone era, including the police box, with police observing the scene and ornate 'bandstand' which actually served as a tram shelter.

The contract for the carriage of school children was too large for Northern Roadways to cope with on their own and some of the work was sub-contracted to a number of other independents with whom they worked closely, including Grant Brothers of Glasgow, who also painted vehicles used in the two tone green livery. Despite its age, CS 124 passed to Grant Brothers and is seen near their garage after sale by Northern Roadways to them in February 1961. Like a few of the Northern Roadways vehicles, it later received a second-hand post-war Alexander body from an ex-Greenock Motor Services/Western SMT Leyland Titan.

Northern continued to buy batches of vehicles for the contract fleet and 14 Leyland Titan TD4s were acquired in 1958/9, rebodied with Alexander utility bodies during the war. All had been built as Leyland Tiger TS7s and were rebuilt as TD4s and rebodied as part of a large programme to increase capacity by Scottish Bus Group members during the war. Leyland Titan CS 2029 is running on hire to SMT in Shettleston Road, with the commonplace Scottish Bus Group paper destination sticker fixed to the nearside lower deck front window, used when a destination display was not available. The canopy above the destination box concealed ventilation slats.

Four pre-war Leyland Titans whose CoFs had expired were acquired for their postwar Alexander bodies in 1959 from Western SMT, all having originated with Greenock Motor Services. Three of them ended up back on ex-Western SMT vehicles, with one being fitted to an ex-Central SMT Leyland TD7. The 1948 Alexander L27/26R body from BU 8428, a 1935 Leyland TD3 acquired from Oldham Corporation and rebodied by Alexander, was grafted onto WJ 9090, a 1934 Leyland TD4, which had originated with Sheffield Corporation and passed to Western SMT via Alexanders. It had already been rebodied once with an Alexander utility body similar to the one illustrated on CS 124, in 1943. Western sold the bus to Millburn Motors in August 1958 and it passed to Northern in the following month. *(Robert Grieves Collection)*

Sister vehicle BU 8429, on the other hand, was purchased from Western via Millburn Motors in September 1958 and operated 'as is'. The similarity of early post-war Alexander bodies to products from Leyland's own bodywork department is striking. To a considerable extent, the composition of Northern's double-deck contract fleet was governed by the disposal programme of Western SMT, who supplied the vast majority of their fleet via Millburn Motors from 1956 until Northern Roadways selling out, over 100 former 'Western' vehicles being operated during that period. Northern were, obviously, happy with the vehicles obtained, given the degree of repeat business.

Although the majority of vehicles from the contract fleet obtained from 1956 were ex-Scottish Bus Group (and, in particular, Western SMT) other sources were tapped for small quantities of vehicles. Four ex-East Yorkshire Leyland PD1s with Roe highbridge bodies (HAT 636, 637, 639-40) were purchased in 1959. They were built with an 'egg shaped' roof to allow them to operate under the Bar Gate in Beverley, through which a number of East Yorkshire's routes passed. HAT 636, operating in the Monklands area and possibly on hire to SMT was a youthful 12 years old which, along with its sister vehicles, made it the most modern double-decker in the fleet.

Vehicles from two non-Scottish Bus Group sources are illustrated, with HAT 640, another of the ex-East Yorkshire Leyland PD1s pictured in the Dalmarnock yard. To its right is YS 2055, one of two ex-Glasgow Corporation Leyland TD4s acquired (the other being YS 2060) which had been rebodied by Alexander in 1949. They were obtained from Park (dealer) Glasgow in 1959. Both carry boards in their lower deck front windows identifying the school duties which they had worked; St Rochs and Easterhouse, plus St Brigid's and Toryglen. *(Robert Grieves Collection)*

Another 'one off' in the fleet was an ex-Southampton Corporation Guy Arab with Park Royal body (DTR 464) which was purchased from North (dealer) Leeds and operated until 1962. The bus is sitting between an ex-Western SMT Guy Arab and one of the relatively long lived ex-Birmingham Daimler COG5s. *(Robert Grieves Collection)*

Along with the TD4s, five Leyland TD5s built in 1938/9 were acquired in 1959, two with Leyland lowbridge bodywork from Yuille of Larkhall, with whom they worked closely and traded vehicles from time to time, which had originated with SMT (BSC 531 and 549). The other three had highbridge bodies and were all ex-Western SMT, CS 7029 (which also came via Yuille) and two via Millburn Motors, CS 8043 and CS 7022 pictured here. Some of these operated for less than a year.

Hutchison of Overtown. Two Plaxton-bodied Bedford SBGs were also acquired from Smith's of Wigan in 1957 and a Duple-bodied Bedford SBO came from Yuille of Larkhall early in 1958.

Eighteen more double-deckers were acquired via Millburn Motors from Western SMT during 1958 allowing further inroads to be made into the ex-Birmingham fleet. Further Guy Arabs were obtained with various makes and configurations of body along with Leyland TD3s and TD4s with wartime Alexander bodies, the latter having been conversions from TS7 single-deckers by Western during the war. Some of this batch operated for less than a year. Double-deckers tended to operate fairly anonymously, other than legal lettering. A few did gain the Northern script fleet name on the sides such as an ex-Western utility Daimler, and an ex-Western Guy Arab which had originated with London Transport and this practice continued on the odd double-decker until the mid-sixties.

Purchases for 1959 included four Leyland PD1s with Roe 'Beverly Bar' style bodies from East Yorkshire, which became the youngest double-deckers in the fleet at twelve years old, along with an ex-Southampton Guy Arab of 1946. Older vehicles also continued to be sourced, two 1935 TD4s rebodied by Alexander in 1949 coming from Glasgow Corporation, three TD5s from Yuille of Larkhall (ex-SOL and Western) and a mixture of TD3s, TD4s (TS7 wartime conversions) and TD5s from Western via Millburn Motors. Four further pre-war Leyland double-deckers were obtained from the same source and these vehicles either donated their post-war Alexander bodies to vehicles already purchased or swapped registrations.

For the first time since 1953 new vehicles were purchased, six Bedford SB3s with Duple bodies being obtained for their coach tour operations, together with one Ford Thames 570E, again with Duple 41-seater coachwork in 1959. This removed the need to hire coaches from other operators.

In 1960, single-deckers were purchased to help to support the contract services, when five Bristol L5Gs with Eastern Coach Works bodies were obtained from Millburn, having originated with the Caledonian Omnibus Company before passing to Western SMT in 1949. Fourteen Leyland TD4s with post-war Northern Counties bodies (including the only one of the batch with standee windows downstairs) were also acquired from Western SMT via Millburn Motors to complete the intake for the year. All the contract fleet vehicles had their destination boxes

painted over and the legend 'private' painted on using a standard stencil. Where specific route information was required for a contract service, a board with the relevant details was generally placed in the nearside lower deck window.

In late 1960 or early 1961 five more Ford Thames 570Es with Duple bodies were purchased new, including one which was displayed in the demonstration park at the Scottish Motor Show. These vehicles appear to have replaced most of the Bedford SB3s purchased in 1959 and lasted around six years. Only two double-deckers, Daimler CVG5s with Northern Counties bodies, were purchased in 1961 and were gone within a year although, as with other vehicles which had very short lives with Northern, they were always painted into the two tone green livery. These Daimlers had started life with Paisley and District Omnibus Service (a company owned by Young's Bus Service, Paisley) in 1947, but had operated for the majority of their life with Western SMT. The licence for the works service between Pollok (Bundy Clock) and Glasgow (Kerr Street) obtained some ten years earlier was surrendered in 1961/2.

Also at this time, another large intake of second-hand vehicles was received via the usual source of Millburn Motors. Further single-deckers arrived in the shape of four ex-Western Guy Arab III single-deckers with Guy bodies new in 1947. It is thought that one of this batch was cut down later into a tow wagon and carried an incorrect 'WG' registration number in this guise. Single-deckers played a bigger part in the contract operations over the next couple of years as the number of school children to be transported reduced.

Western SMT duly disposed of its Northern Counties-bodied AEC double-deckers of 1946 and eight of this batch arrived in late 1961 and early 1962, together with three all-Scottish Albion CX37s with Alexander bodies and seven wartime Guy Arabs (all but one originating with London Transport) with post-war Northern Counties, Alexander or second-hand Croft (of Glasgow) bodies from Western SMT. Eight ex-Ribble Leyland-bodied Leyland PD2s were purchased along with another Roe Beverly Bar style-bodied Leyland PD1 from East Yorkshire and a further Northern Counties-bodied ex-Paisley and District Daimler CVG5 from Western SMT. Alexander (Midland) contributed three Northern Counties-bodied Guy Arabs which had originated with London Transport. Many of the double-deckers from Western and Alexanders arrived in all-over grey, applied to vehicles for

There was a change of emphasis in 1960 with the first purchases of single-deckers for the contract fleet. All five vehicles purchased were new to the Caledonian Omnibus Company Ltd of Dumfries, passing to Western SMT with the absorption of 'Caley' in 1950 and were Bristol L5Gs with Eastern Coach Works bodies. Four of them were relatively youthful, GSM 120 being built in 1946, whilst GSM 123-5 were new in 1947. However, ESM 538, pictured here under maintenance, was new in 1939 and had been rebodied with a similar Eastern Coach Works B35R body to its sister vehicles in 1949, a lowered Bristol radiator being fitted at the same time. *(Garry Ward Collection)*

Along with the single-deckers, the 1960 intake included 14 Leyland TD4s of 1936/7 from the usual source, Western SMT, via Millburn Motors. All had been rebodied in 1949/50 with new Northern Counties L27/26R bodies. They operated for up to two years. CS 4492, near Glasgow Cross, was the only one of the batch to have standee windows fitted (on the nearside only), designed to allow standing passengers a better view of where a bus was on a particular route. Western had sold these vehicles for around £40 per bus to Millburn and, even allowing for dealer 'mark up' would have provided good value for the life of two years or so which they had with Northern Roadways.

Investments had been made in a new coach fleet in 1959, when six Bedford SB3s with Duple C41F bodies were delivered, together with a solitary Ford Thames 570E. Ford found favour with a repeat order for five more Thames 570E models in 1961, registered 64 BYS, 700-1CGA and 94-5 CGD, again with Duple C41F bodies. The Strathpeffer tours operated from Glasgow, as well as private hires, remained an important part of the business. 701 CGA was resting between duties in the silver grey livery, complete with Northern fleet name in the depot yard. *(Alistair Douglas)*

Daimler vehicles returned to the Northern fleet in 1961 when two former Young's Bus Service/Western Daimler CVG5s with Northern Counties H30/26R bodies were purchased. XS 6151, along with XS 6154, were gone within a year.

Four ex-Greenock Motor Services Guy Arab III single-deckers with Guy bodywork formed part of the large intake in 1961/2. All four were purchased during 1961, one having a 34-seater front entrance body (VS 4433) and the other three having B35R bodies (VS 4436, 4651, 4654). The light green relief was limited to around the window areas, applied in a similar style to the ex-Caledonian Bristol L5Gs.

It is almost certain that one of this batch was later converted to a tow wagon. The vehicle was cut down fairly crudely beyond the first bay and had the chassis structure beyond the rear wheels cut away to form the only tow wagon which Northern Roadways possessed. It is probable that it is either VS 4436 or VS 4654 (the WG 8144 registration being incorrect) and it was converted around 1962 when other vehicles were being adapted for GLOCO work, of which more later. *(Robert Grieves Collection)*

Western SMT disposed of their Northern Counties-bodied AEC Regent II's built in 1946 and eight were purchased in late 1961/early 1962 (BAG 124/7, 135-9 and BAG 141). BAG 127 was sitting between CCK 348, one of four ex-Ribble Leyland PD2's purchased in that year and JAT 409, another Roe-bodied Leyland PD1 from East Yorkshire which had been bought in early 1962. It was still in East Yorkshire livery at the time of the photograph, although a painted 'Private' destination had been applied.

Three all-Scottish vehicles were purchased in 1962 in the shape of 1949 Albion Venturer CX37s with Alexander bodies bearing a strong resemblance to Leyland products of the time (CSD 877, 884-5). More youthful than the average age of double-deckers disposed of by Western SMT (15 years was the 'norm' in that period), they would have been even more Scottish had Western not replaced their Albion engines with Gardner engines in the mid 1950's. CSD 884 is carrying a destination suspended from inside the front nearside lower-deck window. These and similarly placed boards were regularly used to identify the schools to which they were operating. Ex-East Yorkshire JAT 409 had gained fleet livery by the time this Albion was photographed and shows, like the ex-Ribble PD2s, the revised livery treatment with the lighter green limited to three bands and the mudguards. As a general rule, previous purchases had the light green applied between decks, with an additional light green band dependent on the style of bodywork. *(Robert Grieves Collection)*

Also acquired in 1962 were seven further Guy Arabs, all wartime chassis and all rebodied with later bodywork by Western SMT. ASD 409 had been new in 1944 but was rebodied in 1949. The new body actually carried a body number under a warranty series issued by Northern Counties and certain parts from the original body including the cab window assembly and more mundane aspects such as stanchion poles were incorporated. The bus was pulling away from a parking spot in Bridgeton Cross in September 1962. *(John Sinclair)*

The other six wartime Guys acquired had originated with London Transport, two carrying second-hand bodies, GLF 661 being an early Guy Arab I model built in 1942, whilst GYL 406 was an Arab II new in 1945. Both had their utility bodies replaced by second-hand Croft Engineering L27/26R bodywork which had been built new in 1947 onto former Caledonian Omnibus Company Leyland Titan TD1s. The now dented extended front dash panel below the drivers' windscreen was an addition by Western SMT to camouflage the effect of the engine bay of the Leyland versus the protruding radiator fitted on the Guy. Behind GLF 661 was BSD 581, one of seven more Guy Arab III's with Guy B33R bodies which had also been acquired in 1962, being converted to an open rear section capable of carrying 'GLOCO' smokeless fuel, in conjunction with a contract which Northern was involved in with DT McFarlane. *(Garry Ward Collection)*

The other four wartime Guy Arabs which had originated with London Transport had been rebodied in 1952 with new Alexander L27/26R bodies. With chassis dating from 1943 GLL 581 had arrived from Millburn Motors, painted in grey 'disposal' primer, a practice which Western SMT adopted from Alexander for a few years in the early 1960s. Other recent arrivals in the grey livery can be seen in the background. The other three wartime Guy Arabs were HGC 155, 197 and 208, all new in 1945.

Millburn Motors had premises at Walmer Bridge, Preston, as well in Glasgow, which made them a convenient sales point for former Ribble vehicles. Many of these came north of the border to the Glasgow depot. Northern bought eight Leyland L27/26R-bodied Leyland PD2/3s, including CCK 366 which was about to take up a contract duty. The bus was built in 1948 and had run as Ribble 2591. Despite the considerable quantity of Ribble vehicles passing through Millburn's hands, they were the only vehicles owned which had originated from this source.

Three former Alexander (Midland) Guy Arabs with Northern Counties H30/26R bodies new in 1945/6 were received in 1962 (GYL 434, 437 and 441). They had originated with London Transport and were similar to three Arabs purchased in 1958, which had originated with Western SMT. Alexander tended to keep their ex-London Transport vehicles for a longer period than Western; these vehicles had operated on the Perth City Services in red livery and had been repainted in all over grey (which was standard Alexander practice) prior to disposal. The three newly acquired vehicles are seen awaiting repaint into Northern colours. *(Robert Grieves Collection)*

disposal by some SBG companies for a period in the early 'sixties. This amounted to an intake of some 34 vehicles in 1962, effectively replenishing the whole contract fleet at that time.

However, there were also more acquisitions during the year from Western SMT (again, via Millburn) which were used for a different purpose. Seven more Guy Arab III single-deckers with Guy 33-seat bodies were acquired and converted into coal storage vehicles for GLOCO smokeless fuel. For this purpose they had their rear ends cut back and adapted to carry the coal with access from the back, windows and side panels painted over and large advert boards fitted to their sides. They were housed in Northern's Dalmarnock yard and were joined by further Northern Roadways' single-deckers including one of the Bristol L5Gs purchased in 1960 and another Arab III single-decker. These vehicles remained for around two-three years and were actually owned by D.T. MacFarlane & Co Ltd., in which Harry McGhee was also a director along with other members of the McGhee family. This had not been Northern's

first involvement in this line of business; after the sale of the express service licences Northern had been involved in the transport of coke from Ayr to Hamilton, using a fleet of 10 to 15 tipper wagons purchased for the purpose. Indeed, Northern Roadways listed their primary role as being both passenger vehicle operators and haulage contractors and they increased their nominal capital again in April 1964 from £12,000 to £25,000.

The large bus intake, not surprisingly, satisfied Northern's vehicle needs for the next two years. When the time came to replenish the stock it comprised the usual mixed bag. Four AEC Regent IIIs with pre-selector gearboxes and Northern Counties bodies were purchased from Western and, interestingly, carried the script Northern fleet name. Two ex-Glasgow Corporation Daimler CVD6 single-deckers with the Corporations' own bodywork arrived, via another Glasgow dealer, Wilmot. An ex-Ribble Leyland TD5 with post war Alexander bodywork came as a non PSV from Holyrood Knitwear of East Kilbride and a wartime Daimler CWA6 with Duple body was purchased from Dundee Corporation.

This small intake was followed by another

BSD 581 is seen after conversion to a store for GLOCO smokeless fuel parked in a corner of the yard, with another of the same batch to the right. The whole batch were converted as fuel carriers (BSD 578, 580-5) and all but one remained licensed until 1964/5, although they do not appear to be intended for movement, given the blanked out drivers cab windows. Large advert boards were carried on the side and front to advertise the fuel, which was a Scottish Gas Board product.

GSM 125 was one of the Bristol L5Gs which had originated with the Caledonian Omnibus Company and had run in the Northern Roadways contract fleet for a year before conversion to a mobile advert vehicle, complete with mock house boarding built around the frame of the bus. Two of the bus side windows have cleverly been incorporated to give the impression of house side windows.

For around three years, there was no requirement for replacement vehicles and when the next acquisitions were made in 1965, the quantities were small. Four Western SMT AEC Regent III's with Northern Counties L27/26R bodies, which had been much liked by the staff of their previous owner, were purchased in April 1965. Unusually, all carried the Northern scroll fleet name which, by then, was rarely applied to vehicles, most running anonymously, except for their legal lettering. They had standee windows downstairs and polished chrome radiators which added to the elegance of these fine vehicles. BSD 446 was, numerically, the second, BSD 444, 449 and 450 being the others of the batch.

Although the numbers of acquisitions in 1965 were small, the variety was considerable. Two ex-Glasgow Daimler CVD6 single-deckers with bodies built by Glasgow Corporation at their Larkfield works seating 33 in 1951/2 were acquired. They had two-door bodies (front entrance, rear exit) with power operated doors, similar to continental practice of the time (the emergency door opening handles can be seen adjacent to each door). Northern had no real requirement for vehicles of this style but, presumably, they obtained a good deal on them through the Glasgow dealer, Wilmot. Either FYS 331 or FYS 342 appeared to be out of service with its seat cushions piled up by the time it was photographed. One of the GLOCO vehicles can just be seen behind it. (Alistair Douglas)

A new source, Dundee Corporation, was also used to acquire one Daimler CWA6 with Duple H30/26R body, YJ 7981, dating from 1944. The bus had yet to be repainted, although legal lettering had been applied. It was parked near the basic office premises which Northern staff used, where a Ford Thames coach was being washed down in preparation for its next duty. *(Alistair Douglas)*

Single-deckers continued to be used to a limited extent in the mid-sixties and some vehicles (both double-deck and single-deck) were operated in their previous livery. CSD 19 was one of four Leyland Tiger PS1s with Alexander C35F bodies which had operated longer lives with Western SMT than normal, running for some 15 years. It ran for less than a year with Northern and the previously applied Northern fleet name can just be discerned as it sits in the premises of Tiger (dealer) Salburgh in September 1967 to the left of an ex-Central SMT (originally Laurie of Hamilton) Leyland PD3 with Northern Counties body.

The biggest intake of former Central SMT vehicles took place with the 1967 purchases of ten Leyland PD1s and PD2s. Although Millburn Motors did trade with Central, these vehicles came from Tiger of Salsburgh, with one coming from Dunsmore of Larkhall. FVD 665 is one of the Leyland PD1s and retained its Central SMT livery, in common with other members of the batch, when captured by the camera hurrying over Bridgeton Cross. By then, the tram tracks and tram and trolleybus wires had gone, although the old tram shelter was still in existence. *(Alistair Douglas)*

Six 'tin front' Guy Arab IVs, Northern's first, were purchased in late 1967/early 1968 and most of them originally operated in Western SMT livery. ESD 210 was one of two built in 1953 (along with sister vehicle ESD 211) and was pulling out of the Dalmarnock yard to begin a contract duty. It wears a later livery adaptation, using the two tone green style, but retaining the cream advert panels it carried in its previous owner's fleet. For a short period, some Northern vehicles carried a fleet number based on the registration number, prefixed by a chassis type code and this can be seen on the bonnet top, ESD 210 carrying the number G210. *(Alistair Douglas)*

The other four Guy Arabs were new in 1955 (GCS 211, 213, 217 and 218) and carried a later, arguably more attractive, upper-deck front window design in its lowbridge body. GCS 213 retained the chrome strip fitted when new down the centre of the radiator, and was numbered G213 with Northern Roadways. The use of the Northern scroll fleet name on a few of the vehicles had ceased by then, identification being limited to a fleet name above the destination box. *(Alistair Douglas)*

In typical Northern Roadways fashion, acquisitions of relatively youthful vehicles were mixed with the purchase of older buses, as always motivated by the availability of a Certificate of Fitness. CCS 404 was one of a batch of Leyland PD1s which had been new in 1948/9, fitted with replacement ECW bodies in 1952 to replace their existing original Strachan ones which had literally fallen apart. It had just left the Dalmarnock yard and was travelling along the old Shettleston Road, with one of the ex-Western SMT 1955 Guy Arabs purchased in 1968 in the background, parked outside the entrance to the yard. (Alistair Douglas)

The other Leyland PD1 (VS 4866) was virtually identical, albeit it had been diverted before delivery to Western's subsidiary Greenock Motor Services and carried a Greenock area registration. This bus, new in 1948, had similarly been rebodied by ECW to replace the original Strachans body. Western's PD1s (rebodied and also those with original Leyland or Northern Counties bodies) had long lives, some lasting nearly 20 years in service. Both PD1s had CoFs which expired in September 1968. *(Alistair Douglas)*

Another of the batch, JCS 430 is seen with earlier acquired Guy GSD 701 (one of six Guys acquired in 1969/70, the others being GSD 695, 699, 702-4), and one of the two tin front Leyland PD2/20s HCS 997 (also purchased in 1971, along with fellow HCS 993) parked behind. By the time of this view in August 1971, the fleet had moved to much smaller premises at 332 Edinburgh Road, Glasgow. *(John Sinclair)*

Ford coaches remained popular with Northern Roadways in the late 'sixties. After the purchase of two Ford R192's with Duple 45-seater bodies from Happiway-Spencer in 1969 (GVU 74E new in 1967 and JVM 473F new in the following year), another 1968 Ford R192, LSN 713F, this time with Plaxton C45F body was purchased in 1970 from Barrie of Balloch. (Alistair Douglas)

small quantity of vehicles in 1966. The coaching fleet was upgraded with a two year old Ford Thames 570E, followed by three two-year-old Bedford SB5s with Duple Bella Vega bodies in the following year from the Happiway-Spencer Group, Manchester. Their blue livery was adopted for the coach fleet at the same time, thus ending the silver livery worn by the coaches since early post-war days. Single-deckers were still being used to an extent and four 1949/50 Leyland Tiger PS1s with Alexander bodywork were purchased from Western SMT via Millburn in 1966.

A mixture of ten Leyland Titans (both PD1s and PD2s ranging from 1948 to 1952) were acquired from Central SMT in 1967 via Tiger of Salsburgh, with one coming from Dunsmore of Larkhall. Both were dealers who scrapped buses and undertook some reselling. A single 20-year old Leyland PD1 was obtained from the more usual source of Western SMT via Millburn Motors. In later 1967 and early 1968, the fleet was further topped up with six ex-Western SMT Guy Arab IVs, built in 1953 or 1955. Some of these vehicles were operated in Western's red livery and carried

a simple Northern fleet name in capitals above the lower-deck windows. A few of the vehicle wore fleet numbers, linked to their chassis type and registration number; thus, DVD 268 an ex-Central SMT Leyland PD2 carried fleet number L268, whilst GCS 213, a Guy Arab IV from Western, carried number G213. Further acquisitions continued in 1968 with two ECW-rebodied Leyland PD1s arriving from Western via Millburn and eight more Leyland PD2s being purchased from Central SMT via Tiger of Salsburgh.

Thus, 28 more double-deckers were purchased between 1967 and 1968 to form the core of the contract fleet, some way off the 60 or so vehicles operated in the mid 'fifties, but still substantial. These marked the last big purchases and the fleet reduced considerably in the following years with a much smaller intake of vehicles. The registered office had moved on two further occasions with the movement of Harry McGhee's solicitor's office, to 45 Renfield Street in October 1959 and 26B Renfield Street in May 1968.

From 1969, the contract fleet mostly remained in their previous operator's colours. In practice, this meant Western SMT livery. Four more Guy Arab IVs, dating from 1956, with Alexander L31/28RD bodies, were obtained in 1971 (JCS 6, 8,10, 430). JCS 6 was the last double-decker in the Northern Roadways fleet, surviving until 1976. Ahead of JCS 6 is JCS 10 which was repainted in a brighter red livery with cream window surrounds. It was withdrawn, along with the other two of the batch in 1973. *(John Sinclair)*

Two more Leyland PD2s arrived from Central SMT in 1969, followed by six more ex-Western SMT Guy Arab IVs with NCME bodies in 1969 and 1970. Two Ford R192s with Duple C45F bodies were acquired from Happiway-Spencer, having served around two years with their original owners and these were joined by a similar example, but with Plaxton bodywork, from Barrie of Balloch in 1970.

The Final Days

Around 1970 much of the remaining contract double-deck fleet was disposed of and Northern moved their much reduced fleet to correspondingly smaller premises at the rear of a petrol station at 332 Edinburgh Road, Glasgow, not far from Calderpark Zoo. They shared the yard with vehicles of Wallace Arnold of Leeds, used on their Scottish tours programme. Their last purchases of ex-Scottish Bus Group stock were made in 1971 with two 1956 'tin front' Leyland PD2s with NCME bodies and four Alexander-bodied Guy Arab IVs of the same age from Western SMT, via Millburn Motors as usual. One of these, JCS 10, was repainted red with cream window surrounds, but the remainder operated in Western livery of dark red with cream bands. All lasted around the usual two years except JCS 6 which operated until the demise of the company in 1978. Prior to the arrival of the last SBG vehicles a few of the contract vehicles operated in an adaptation of the standard scheme of green, relieved with cream.

Three small Bedford C5Z1s with Duple 29-seat coach bodies were acquired from MacBraynes in 1971 and served until 1976 and 1977. Northern returned to new-coach purchases in 1973 with a Ford R1014 45-seater bodied by Plaxton and finished in an orange and light blue livery, followed by a similar example in 1974. In that year, John Anderson McGhee resigned, being replaced by Ronald B McGhee. Another Plaxton-bodied Ford was purchased in 1976 to replace the 1973 example and a 1973 Willowbrook-bodied Ford 48-seater arrived in the same year, ex-Newton of Dingwall.

For the much-reduced contract operations, four Bristol Lodekkas (the only vehicles of this type owned), were purchased in 1971 and 1972 from Crosville.

The Ellerman Travel Group acquired Northern Roadways and Travel Trips Ltd, together with the Ben Wyvis Hotel, in November 1978, and the remaining small fleet was sold. By then, Harry McGhee had resigned. Prior to this, Northern's registered office had moved to Bishop & Co, 133 St Vincent Street, Glasgow in November 1977. Ellerman's principle interest was in the hotel and travel agency but both companies remained under the portfolio owned by Ellerman Travel and Leisure Ltd.. The remaining members of the McGhee family (Alistair McGhee and Ronald B McGhee, who was also company secretary) resigned as directors in March 1979 and the registered office made it's final move to Ellerman Travel and Leisure Ltd., 221 West George Street, Glasgow in April 1981. Northern Roadways Ltd was finally dissolved in July 1983, thus ending a relatively short but very eventful existence. Travel Trips survived longer, finally being dissolved in 1989. Although Ellerman Travel is no more, the impressive looking Ben Wyvis Hotel remains in operation, a fitting memorial to a company that had an eventful life.

Acknowledgements

From the foregoing it will be appreciated that there are still gaps in this often complex story, as indicated in the introduction, but the author hopes that enough information has been given to provide a picture of this interesting company and maybe to prompt others who may have knowledge that could be shared.

Those that have helped to bring the story to this point are sincerely thanked. Two former employees who drove on the express services, Jimmy Conner and Bill McDonald, patiently helped with much valuable information on these operations. Others who deserve special thanks for their help with photographs, information or both are Ian MacLean, Alistair Douglas, George Heaney, Graham Ewing, Adrian and Gerald Hamill, the late Ron Logan, Robert Grieves, Richard Gadsby,

MacBrayne became a new source for vehicles with the purchase in 1971 of three small Bedford C5Z1's with Duple 29-seat bodies. They were actually purchased from Highland Omnibuses, who had absorbed MacBraynes' operations into their fleet. They provided useful smaller vehicles for hiring work and Bedford YYS 175, along with YYS 177 and 609 CYS ran until 1976/7. *(Alistair Douglas)*

Examples of the later Ford 1014 with Plaxton 45-seat bodies were purchased new in 1973, 1974 and 1976. HGB 151L was the 1973 delivery, complete with illuminated Northern Roadways fleet name side panel and it carried a new orange and light blue livery. Although HGB 151L was sold in 1976, the other two Fords bought new (JDS 644N and NGD 971P) survived until Northern Roadways and its associated companies sold out in 1978. Another Ford (SJS 37L) acquired from Newton of Dingwall, to replace the last double-decker in 1976, also survived until the end and all three were later sold to Salopia of Whitchurch. *(Alistair Douglas)*

the late Geoff Morant, John C Gillham, John Sinclair, David Mitchell, Alan Cross and Tom McMorland. I have credited the photographs used where known and apologise in advance for any who have been inadvertently missed or are simply unknown. Sources of information have included the commercial press, Minute Books of Western SMT, and PSV Circle records and the Omnibus Society Library at Ironbridge, plus some recently uncovered archive material, supplementing my own researches. To all of these sources and any that I have inadvertently missed, I extend my grateful thanks.

Venture Publications editorial team and readers have worked hard to bring my work into a form suitable for publication and I thank Ian Stubbs for handling the layout. David and Mary Shaw meticulously read the proofs but any errors which have slipped through are mine and not theirs.

Finally, I must thank Caroline who has continued to support me in the hobby that 'chose me'; without her encouragement, interest and patience, I would not have completed this project or continued with other research in between the many other calls of family life which compete for my time.

Scottish Aviation bodied AEC Regal FGG 171 is photographed with Fred Newton of Conan Bridge, to whom this coach passed from Northern Roadways in the early fifties